indomitable

indomitable

A FOSTER CARE STORY

Di Ciruolo

NEW YORK

LONDON • NASHVILLE • MELBOURNE • VANCOUVER

indomitable

a foster care story

© 2024 Di Ciruolo

Published in New York, New York, by Morgan James Publishing. Morgan James is a trademark of Morgan James, LLC. www.MorganJamesPublishing.com

Proudly distributed by Publishers Group West®

Morgan James BOGO™

A **FREE** ebook edition is available for you or a friend with the purchase of this print book.

CLEARLY SIGN YOUR NAME ABOVE

Instructions to claim your free ebook edition:
1. Visit MorganJamesBOGO.com
2. Sign your name CLEARLY in the space above
3. Complete the form and submit a photo of this entire page
4. You or your friend can download the ebook to your preferred device

ISBN 9781636980942 paperback
ISBN 9781636980959 ebook
Library of Congress Control Number: 2022948798

Cover Design by:
Rachel Lopez
www.r2cdesign.com

Interior Design by:
Christopher Kirk
www.GFSstudio.com

Morgan James is a proud partner of Habitat for Humanity Peninsula and Greater Williamsburg. Partners in building since 2006.

Get involved today! Visit: www.morgan-james-publishing.com/giving-back

To all the kids who didn't survive the foster care system.
To those we lost and keep losing to negligence, apathy, selfishness, narcissism, and greed.
You didn't disappear. It wasn't your fault. You were never the problem.
And I didn't forget.

The truth is like a lion.
You don't have to defend it.
Let it loose, and it will defend itself.
—Augustine

How to Read

I don't remember being a child. That's not to say I don't have memories from childhood. I do. What I mean to say is, I don't remember them the way we think a child might. I think it's that way for a lot of people with trauma. I remember memories as a tiny adult. Or at least someone who had to take her own survival as seriously as any adult may. Children often think they are immortal. Adults know better. So did I.

Human memory is interesting, especially as we take child development into account. I hadn't given it a lot of thought until I had my own children, but I've had many psychologists muse at my "origin story."[1] I've been told that, indeed, young children do have episodic memories, but usually forget them upon reaching adolescence. It's called "childhood amnesia." Furthermore, I've been challenged on that with the fact that a lot of adults seem to think their memories are from earlier than they can be—but aren't.[2] But after reconnecting with my birth father as an adult, I found an apartment I kept remembering, and accurately described, was a place we'd been evicted from when I was eighteen months old and when

---

1 My friend Katrina Strohl called my background my origin story on her podcast *Absolutely Not!*, and obviously I'm keeping it.
2 Scientific American Mind, "When Do Children Start Making Long-Term Memories?," *Scientific American*, December 8, 2016, https://doi.org/10.1038/scientificamericanmind0117-72a.

my brother Ted would've been five months old. I don't know why that's true, but I get it's *different*.

Honestly, I think early traumatic experiences "brought me online" a little earlier than researchers might see in average children. There's never any new research on people like me between the times that I check, but I guess *who are they going to ask? Me?*

I say that because there are people in this story who don't come off so great. Sometimes I'll be one of those people. I was a very defiant teenager, for example. My ADHD compounded that. And in my hurt, I've said some things to people that I wish I could unsay. But I've been carrying 100 percent of the guilt for every little thing that happened as if I were a full adult participant with full agency in this story rather than a child who was the victim of a terrible system and an almost unbelievable number of callous and apathetic adults.

I've been adultifying my traumatized child behavior.

And in order to live, I need to stop doing that. In order to climb any higher in my life, I need to put this down first. I need to find peace.

That being said, it was not an easy choice to write this story.

A cultural rule of foster care is that you never tell someone else's story. Our stories and our experiences are all we have, and we share them with each other to build the trust and relationships we were denied in our own birth families. This is true for abandoned queer kids too.

You can always tell when a book uses foster care as a trope because it's obvious the writer spent no time in the foster care system. *This isn't one of those stories.*

None of my story was happening to me alone. And I've spent years struggling with how to do the story justice without hurting anyone else who was just there, like me. I've kept silent for that reason for so long, but I'm tired of the lies. I'm tired of the euphemisms. I'm tired of the predators joking about sex trafficking while wearing fancy clothes at "nice" parties.

*I'm tired of people who have been given countless advantages in life telling other people how to **work** for what they were **given**.*

As if they know.

I'm tired of asking fancy charities what help they are providing to the roughly half a million foster kids in the US and being met with blank stares and embarrassed vamping. I think if the kids who were around then and living this way with me were still around today, they'd be just as sick of this as I am. But they aren't. They're dead. Or in prison. Or trying to die.

I've always felt that that empty space should be held in memory, but now I see that my silence isn't doing that.

I only know three people who were in foster care who are currently "thriving," and they weren't in homes with me. I met them on my travels. I'm one of the three.

If you get put into foster care for any reason, your chances of graduating from high school have just been cut to 50 percent. For graduating from college, that's 3 percent. If you go to a junior college first and then try to go to a four-year school like they tell you to do, you will almost certainly drop out with no degree. And yet, we keep pretending that's a real avenue for kids who have no parental support or resources to pull themselves out of debilitating poverty while meeting impossible mental health crises.

I'll be hiding names and context throughout this book as much as possible. And I know I'll anger people. But every year there seems to be less and less space for me to hide from this. Every year there seem to be fewer survivors exiting the system and more and more victims coming into it, regardless. The box I share with this story is getting too small for me to breathe.

I waited for someone else, anyone else, to come out and say what needs to be said. I made every excuse for why I shouldn't be the one to write this book. I did everything else first. I tried to fit in every box that I even remotely had an interest in, and I outgrew every box quickly.

It can't be me.

But that's the thing about being called to do something as insane as reliving this story for public consumption—I can't run from it. I have *tried*. Please believe I've started and stopped this book one hundred times in my life, always knowing I would one day have to give an account of this in some way. That's a big thing to know.

Some of this will seem totally unbelievable for people who haven't had these experiences, and for some others, it will be like I was living in your home with you.

I'm choosing life, not just for me but for you. For the kids who are still in the system. For my kids. For my partner. For all of us. So we can all survive. So we can build the blueprint for thriving together.

Another part of the story I'll be sharing for context comes from my most frequently received question:

"How did you survive?"

I'm going to try to reflect on that a lot throughout. I have my own theories, and, quite frankly, I think I'm right. But I don't know what I can't see, so I'm going to try to be as forthright as I can be when remembering and retelling this massive story. What if this is a cheat code I've been given that only makes sense when others view it? I don't know. But I'm hopeful.

I'm going to tell the story and also try to give my inner monologue or any feelings I'm experiencing from my point of view. As a function of ADHD, my brain will need to remember the story literally, as it happened, feelings and all. That can be terrible for the remembering but can be a real measure for truth, so I'll leave it in.

But where I can, I am also going to reflect as my adult self in the story to keep a steady voice, so to speak, for those who have experienced trauma. If you see yourself in my story, I want you to see how I survived it with your own lens. I think I see it all, but maybe you can see a little more if I'm as honest as I can be.

I used to think of this story as a wet, sticky ball of hair that I had to keep inside my chest at all times. Remember the oil that leaked out of the spray paint in *FernGully*?[3] It looks and moves like that. As a child, I used to think I was the person who was supposed to remember. And that I couldn't tell it to people because then they would be stained by it too. It was my job to bear it. My job to survive it.

---

3   *FernGully: The Last Rainforest*, directed by Bill Kroyer (1992; Los Angeles, CA: 20th Century Fox, 2005), DVD.

The one time I started telling some of my story to someone I was dating, he sat in his mother's white Lexus SUV listening for a little while, and then after about five minutes of my talking, he got out of the car and puked on the side of the road while I watched frozen in an absolute shame spiral of horror.

I recognize now that he's just a narcissist,[4] but back then I thought *I* was disgusting, dirty, and bad.

Unworthy.

Upon thirty years of reflection and obsessive remembering of the story, it occurred to me: maybe this isn't just *my* story. Maybe it's just my job to catalog and carry the messages until I can give them back. Maybe I can tell it and finally put it down. Maybe I can do other things. Maybe I can dream for things.

I hope so.

In my lifetime of conversations as the only foster kid anyone ever knew, I can tell you two absolutely true facts about foster care: most people have never considered (1) how heinous the foster care system must be as a result of nearly constant budget cuts, and (2) what the consequences of apathy are when we consider the roughly half a million kids in foster homes or on parenting plans with the Department of Children and Family Services (DCFS) in the US at any given time.

People think foster kids are a burden on society, and it shows. Especially in times when we as humans are all trying to survive the unprecedented.

A few things: Did you know that any social program money that could go to supporting parents who are struggling goes instead to remove children and put them in foster care, and there just isn't the money to check on them enough? Did you know they garnish already impoverished parents' wages to recoup those costs?[5] Did you know that children who end up in foster care due to the death of their parents who are eligible for social security benefits in

---

4   Of course, I'll get to him later.
5   Joseph Shapiro, Teresa Wiltz, and Jessica Piper, "States Send Kids to Foster Care and Their Parents the Bill — Often One Too Big to Pay," NPR, December 27, 2021, https://www.npr.org/2021/12/27/1049811327/states-send-kids-to-foster-care-and-their-parents-the-bill-often-one-too-big-to-.

some cases, regularly have the system apply for those benefits "on their behalf" to try to claw back monies the state put out for foster care? It's true.[6]

And then somehow, people assume I was abandoned for cause, rather than removed.

In my opinion, this victim blaming is present in all discussions of systemic issues that people think are "too big to solve." Who I am can be very triggering for people because they think of systemic problems as being far away or happening to other kids. So when they meet me, they go through a kind of grieving process that they seem to feel I'm responsible for. This process ultimately lands on blaming the victim without intending to by casual use of expressions people always say but never reflect on.

As a child, I was technically and legally a ward of the Commonwealth of Massachusetts until I "aged out" and became homeless.

I am the Daughter of the Commonwealth.

I was removed from my enormous Hispanic family, and the foster care agencies that the state was contracting care out to at the time literally never bothered to reach out to *any* of them.

When my grandmother tried to get benefits to care for me, she was refused and told she was too old. When my twenty-year-old aunt tried to do the same, she was too young. I would later find out my father's father is one of ten siblings living in the US. Ten. My aunties are only in their seventies now and I'm nearly forty. But those resources somehow weren't available for my family. Only for the horrifically abusive homes DCFS sent me to.

I know DCFS didn't check on me, or even inspect the homes I was in, because one of them from that day to this is owned by a narcissistic hoarder with full-blown mental illness, and several rooms in her home are filled from floor to ceiling with garbage and dead rodents. How does *that* happen if you're checking?

---

6   Eli Hager and Joseph Shapiro, "State Foster Care Agencies Take Millions of Dollars Owed to Children in Their Care," NPR, April 22, 2021, https://www.npr.org/2021/04/22/988806806/state-foster-care-agencies-take-millions-of-dollars-owed-to-children-in-their-ca.

It happened because people felt it was a nice house in a nice area with a nice family. It was already *more than I deserved* as a foster kid. They told me all the time.

Better than where you were, right?

I talk a lot about the fact that I attract narcissists. I have dealt with an inordinate number of narcissists in my life. Narcissism's hallmarks are an inflated ego, a lack of empathy, and a need for attention, but how narcissists behave in life is more than that. A narcissist thinks everyone is "out to get them" because they are "out to get" others. *Every accusation is a confession.*

They imagine they are smarter than everyone else and are just moving people around the board to the narcissist's own benefit. As if every person in their life were just a tool to use to their greatest advantage. Especially their children. They are experts at playing the victim in situations they created. They surround themselves with enablers who know the narcissist *must be lying*, but enablers hope they can benefit by sitting at the right hand of the devil rather than in his path, so to speak. They are experts at gaslighting. They use what we call the "invisible army" strategy, which is when they say things like "many people agree with me that I am the victim here!" thus invoking their own "invisible army."

They are experts at finding a person's weak spot and usually prefer to target folks with trauma backgrounds. The path of manipulation and control for a narcissist is to "love bomb" a new target or love interest.[7] The narcissist becomes completely involved in everything about you, pretending to be whatever you said you wanted in a relationship to hook you. Then, when you're already involved with them, they start to pull back their attention from you and start not responding to texts or outreach, and then they start acting like you're crazy for questioning whether anything is wrong. Then you start chasing them as a result of your (likely) trauma background. And then they play little games with you and their enablers. They separate you from your friends and family because you're easier to control if you're just you. And ADHD-ers attract narcissists.

---

7   They don't love others, only themselves.

It's important to me that you know I survived what you're about to read.

I didn't live these moments all at once, and there's an enormous cost to retelling them. They are and can be very triggering for anyone with a trauma history, so please:

Don't read it all at once.

CAST

My Birth Family:
Kate: My birth mother.

Eddie: My birth father. He's in radio now.

Ted: My younger middle brother, rumored to be a half-brother.

Kyle: My youngest half-brother; Donnie's son.

Other Actors:
Donnie: Kate's first boyfriend after my father; Kyle's father.

Sandy: Donnie's biological daughter; Kyle's other half-sister.

Bud: Kate's first boyfriend after Donnie.

Carly: Foster mother of the Trailer.

Luke: Carly's son, who had to be locked in his room at night.

Monica: Carly's longest foster daughter, who abused with Luke.

The Smiths: A Foster Family
Karen: The foster mother.

Willy: The foster father; Karen's husband.

Keith: The eldest child in the foster family.

Peggy: Keith's first wife.

Mae: Keith's second wife.

Marie: The eldest daughter. A frequent victim of Karen's abuse.

Jessica: Marie's daughter.

Will: The second eldest son of the foster family.

Molly: The mother of Will's first child, a daughter.

Lolly: The mother of Will's second child, a son. (Yep, their names really rhyme.)

Neil: The youngest biological son.

Ted: My brother who was in the foster family with me.

Becky: The youngest foster daughter, who is six years younger than me.

Chavonne: The youngest biological daughter, who is seven years younger than me.

The O'Briens: A Boyfriend's Family

Todd: The boyfriend.

Mr. Big: The dad.

Polly: The mom.

(Plus two sisters with whom I have no beef.)

Mason Street (2020)

My partner starts the car.

"You just tell me how to get there, and I'll just sit there," he says, his voice even.

I nod, emotionally preparing myself for the callous stupidity of what I'm about to do.

Can't do this.

I'm riding to the Duplex. One of the scariest places in my child-memory. The hairy edges of which I try endlessly not to acknowledge. But it's always there. That's the thing about trauma. It doesn't go anywhere unless you process it. You don't forget.

Time doesn't heal anything on its own.

"Drive like you're going to the hospital, and then go right after the high school," I instruct tightly.

Definitely not the voice I create in. Not the voice I mother in. Not the voice I think in. There's a tightening in my chest. I can feel my breathing being constricted by the racing in my heart. I can feel pain starting from under my ribs and exploding over my chest to form a tightening knot in my throat. Anxiety.

Stop!

I feel my legs tightening at the thighs as the adrenaline hits, and I grab the door handle to steady my breathing. I don't want my partner to see what this is costing me. I don't want him to worry. He's a worrier. And I have to do this very stupid thing. My brain has gone into full ADHD-chanting mode:

No. No. No. No. No. NO. NO.

I start self-soothing, out loud, to compensate.

"You've totally got this. We're going to do it. You have nothing to be afraid of," I say aloud.

My partner "pulls me out" to ask for directions.

He points left. I nod.

"It's this one," I say, pointing to the street.

"Are you sure?" he asks. "You said it was Swan . . .?"

"It's that one," I mutter, feeling nausea build.

He nods, silently takes a left across traffic onto the street, and parallel parks evenly.

Somewhere in the part of my brain still capable of rational thought, I congratulate myself for remembering there's parallel parking here and that would've required all of my brain. As would driving here. In fact, we only made it because I'm too stubborn to back out, and I wasn't capable of communicating a lengthy but rational reason to do so on the way.

It's drizzling. And cold. A woman who doesn't recognize us peeks out from her front steps three houses down. She stares at me, no doubt asking the question every elderly person asks when they look out: *Who are you, and what are you doing here?*

I'm not staying, I think as loudly as I can.

She seems to give up and goes inside, probably deciding the random pair in the green Subaru don't have much in the way of bad intentions. She's wrong. This is absolutely insane. I've no idea what's going to happen, or if I can manage the damage my mental health will sustain every moment I have to sit there. My memories leak poison like radiation into my system. My partner slides his seat back and pretends to read emails and not be worried.

I open my journal and sketch the outside of the house.

"I remember that door being thicker," I muse to myself aloud.

Then, as I draw the layout of the inside of the house from memory—from over thirty years ago—a light comes on inside on the left side of The Duplex where we didn't live.

"That's the living room on the other side of the house," I almost whisper. "It's laid out the same but opposite on both sides."

I look down at the very specific light fixture I had just sketched now being illuminated in this stranger's living room. It's still the same after thirty years.

Fine, I concede as the tears start to fall. I put my AirPods in and press play on the song. The song I can't hear without being ill. The song that plays in my mind during all memories of the place I have stupidly returned to after promising my inner child we would never ever come back. Here we are again in the broad light of day. It's finally time to remember what happened here.

Fine. I'll remember you. I'll write it down this once, and then we'll never talk about it again.

Live to Tell

I remember moving into Donnie's house, which is about thirty minutes outside of Boston, Massachusetts, in a relatively nondescript suburban town, not unlike those you would find anywhere around the United States. He lived on one side of a duplex home.

I would have been three years old at this point. I remember he had a daughter my age, Sandy. She didn't live with him. He treated her like a princess the one time she came to visit. I remember being very jealous that she got to see her dad because my dad did not live with us anymore and I missed him a lot.

The only thing I remember about that day was that we were playing a game that required us to flip a coin to see who would go first. I'd never seen someone flip a coin before, so I thought the job was to catch the quarter once he dropped it after it rolled away. I ran to retrieve it for him, and he backhanded me across the mouth "for cheating" and "trying to make [*his*] daughter lose."

That was the only time Sandy visited while I was living there. I found out later that Sandy's mom was already trying to keep Donnie away from Sandy because she had already caught him sexually abusing her. Apparently, she was ashamed to tell people and just kicked him out and kept him away without reporting it to the police. *Or anyone.*

My youngest brother, Kyle, told me once that Donnie paid child support *to his daughter for her children.* I asked him why that was.

"I'm afraid to ask," he'd answered.

Donnie taught guitar lessons to children in town and, at the time we were living with him, was in an eighties cover band. I remember the lead singer in that band was really kind to me. She was dating one of the other members, but she hid me behind her back one time when Donnie and my mother, Kate, were shaming me in front of their bandmates. The singer was sitting on a barstool and just pulled me into her arms and said, "It's okay, no one can see you."

At that time, the band was practicing the song "Live to Tell" by Madonna. Donnie sang backup vocals for that song, and I remember hearing the melody, the foreboding lyrics in the weight of his dark presence in my life; it scared me to death. It was warning me of something I didn't have context for yet.

". . . hope I live to tell the secret I have learned, til then it will burn inside of me"[8]

I knew I could die there, and that Donnie would hurt me if I ever gave him the chance. I knew it at three years old. I also knew my mother wouldn't protect me. And I knew Ted, my younger middle brother who was born with drug and fetal alcohol syndrome, was still nonverbal and would surely die without me.

Do you know what the abuse rate for people with disabilities is? Data suggests more than ninety percent of people with developmental disabilities will experience sexual abuse at some point in their lives.[9] And, with an estimated 291 million children and adolescents with disabilities[10] (and it's likely that's underreporting), it doesn't take a math whiz to understand just how many of our vulnerable population are being abused.

---

8   Madonna, "Madonna - Live to Tell (Official Video)," YouTube, July 3, 2011, https://www. youtube.com/watch?v=IzAO9A9GjgI.

9   Valenti-Hein, D. & Schwartz, L. (1995). *The Sexual Abuse Interview for Those with Developmental Disabilities.* James Stanfield Company. Santa Barbara: California

10   Fran Kritz, "A Report on Violence against Kids with Disabilities Is Sobering — If Not Surprising," NPR, April 12, 2022, sec. Goats and Soda, https://www.npr.org/sections/goa tsandsoda/2022/04/12/1091679303/a-report-on-violence-against-kids-with-disabilities-is-sobering-if-not-surprisin.

". . . if I ran away, I'd never have the strength to go very far . . ."

One of the worst things about living with Donnie was the change that came over my mother. I remember thinking that when my mother and father were married, my mother loved me, and I was her daughter. But when we came to live with Donnie, something changed in her and she could hardly stand the sight of me.

"Machado's bastard daughter," Donnie had called me, even though my parents *were* married, and even though she'd gotten pregnant to force him to marry her. That's how abuse is. It doesn't have to be true, and it's usually about the abuser.

I was **tortured** constantly.

One of my punishments was to clean the kitchen floor with my bare hands. I'd be under the table as he ate, trying to brush up the crumbs with my three-year-old hands. I remember vividly where my fear of spiders came from. Under that filthy table. My mother was *delighted* to have inspired a fear in me and would pull the legs off daddy longlegs and throw them on my bed when she found them. She and Donnie gleefully told me that the eyes of spiders sit on top of the legs, watch each leg, and are watching me in my bed at night.

Another punishment was starvation.

Under Donnie's influence, my mother started starving me. When Donnie didn't like something I'd done, which was always, they'd decide together not to feed me. He delighted in her worst impulses, often praising her more. I would daily be standing in the corner alone, except for the spiders, until bedtime.

It's hard to describe to someone what starvation feels like if they don't know. But it feels like screaming in your head. It feels like your body is cannibalizing your muscles and your bones to stay alive. Because it is. The headaches will stab into your brain trying to alarm you into eating. Your best bet is to lie in a fetal position and pray for the sleep that eventually comes from weakness and exhaustion. But on nights when I couldn't ignore the hunger, when the hunger overpowered my self-preservation instincts, I would sneak out of the room I shared with my younger brother to find food. Sometimes I was lucky and I would find partially rotten food on the stove or kitchen table. Sometimes not.

On one particularly memorable night, I found Kraft mac and cheese on the stove that I couldn't quite reach, and I had to drag the heavy kitchen chair to the stove and just eat it as fast as I could before they could catch me. They came.

"You sneaky piece of s—t!" Donnie shouted.

"How dare you?!" Kate screamed.

I stood shaking in fear, crying hysterically, held in place by Donnie's huge hand. And that's when my mother decided to show him *just how loyal she could be*. Remembering her own abuse, she went to the cabinet for the Tabasco sauce, grabbed me by the back of my long hair, and poured the Tabasco sauce down my throat. I vomited up what I'd managed to eat, scream-crying at this point, as they laughed. She threw me into the vomit and told me to "clean up [my] mess." Then they went and had sex. That became one of their favorite ways to hurt me *together*. A bonding ritual. One would hold me down and the other would hold my nose until I opened my mouth and they'd laugh and laugh. I was left to clean up my own vomit and they'd go off together. That was her reward for hurting her own three-year-old daughter. Sexual attention from him.

I tell you this first so you understand, as I did, how important it was that I not get caught. When you're being slowly starved to death by your own mother, the only thing that matters is staying alive and keeping your brother alive too. I became more desperate. I didn't want to leave my brother alone with them. He wasn't as strong as I was.

Every night that I snuck out of my room, I had to drink water from the toilet with my hands.

I'd tested out Donnie's and my mother's response rates to bathroom noises: toilet flushing, tap running. Using Ted's potty chair and drinking from the toilet were the only way to stay alive. I still feel some shame at telling that story. But as a mother of a daughter who looks just like I did, I can say with complete authority: *the shame was absolutely theirs*.

I was being raised by a mother who fawned at violence, which would lead to sexual situations with men for her.

Donnie walked around the house fully naked.

He'd often trap me in the bathroom, while he was naked and I was alone, so I avoided being in the bathroom whenever possible. If I was washing my hands, he'd brush himself on my body behind me. If I was peeing, he'd ask whether we could share. When I told my mother, she told me it was "his house." He was renting it. That's how poor we were. He could be a renter and he was above us.

When they went out of town for shows for his band, they left us locked in our bedroom with a TV set to PBS and a potty chair. No food. No one.

I would lie on the bed on my side, starving, and watch *Sesame Street*, *Mister Rogers' Neighborhood*, and *Reading Rainbow* and pretend they were my family. I still think of LeVar Burton as my TV dad.

My younger brother was two and he wasn't as practiced as me. Usually she fed him. He was still a baby, after all. I'm sure I harbored resentment at that, at least to some extent. Why did she just hate me? But he hadn't escaped their willful neglect this time. They left him in a diaper and left me to watch him with no food. He cried so pitifully. At first, I remember wishing he'd shut up, but I heard in my heart even as young as I was that I didn't want that. I knew when I was three that I didn't want him to stop crying because that would mean he hadn't made it, and I needed to make sure he made it.

He begged me to call for our mother.

"Please," he whispered. "Please call Mumma."

But I didn't. Because I knew if I called, she wouldn't come. She had never come before, and I knew she was gone. I knew she didn't care. I was so afraid he wouldn't live if I wasn't lending my support to him physically. I let him sleep next to me even though he was wet and soiled.

My mother worked nights for a convenience store in town, which used to be in a little shopping center near a Domino's Pizza. They moved it down the street, but it was within walking distance. While Kate didn't protect me from

Donnie ever (and was usually the one doing the hurting, anyway), I was more afraid of him than I was of her. Marginally.

One such night, Donnie had invited me to sit on the couch with him while he smoked cigarettes and watched *Jaws*, knowing I'm scared to death of sharks but not letting me cover my eyes. I still remember trying to cover my face with the afghan from the couch when he grabbed me by my long ponytail and put out his cigarette on my back. I screamed and cried and ran for the door. I assume I was hoping to run to my mother. In my childhood memory, the door is big and thick, and he keeps his keys in the deadbolt, and you have to turn the keys to open the door, but my fingers are too small and not strong enough to turn the key over the lock to escape. He grabs me by my hair and drags me to my room and beats me until I'm unconscious. I have a perfect circle-shaped scar on my right shoulder to this day. I tell people it's a chicken pox scar. I don't always have the heart to teach someone a lesson about minding their own business. Sometimes I just want an interaction to be over.

When I was just four, I found out why Donnie wasn't allowed to see his daughter anymore.

My mother was working that night, and it was unusually hot for Massachusetts. It must have been early summer because Kyle was born midway through July and she was still pregnant. Kyle is Donnie's son.

I had just moved into my new "big girl" room away from Ted, who stayed in the "baby room." I was so excited to be big. I really looked forward to helping with the new baby. I remember before my mother left that night, she told me to clean my room extra good and not bother Donnie. She told me that if I didn't want him to hurt me, I had to clean, make no noise, and help out with Ted. To some extent, I still felt that we were allies. Against him maybe? Or at least I knew she was afraid of him too. I saw her as someone successfully evading the torture he was killing me with, so I did *try* to take her advice.

But let me let you in on an adult trauma survivor secret: ***an abuser will always find an excuse.*** And a sexual abuser will ***always find an opportunity*** to create a new victim. Always. And it isn't your fault. The shame is theirs.

That's why grooming[11] is often such a central part of each person's sexual abuse story. The shame from the idea that you are complicit in your own abuse permeates the mind in a kind of dual consciousness.[12]

"A man can tell a thousand lies, I've learned my lesson well. Hope I live to tell the secret I have learned, 'til then? It will burn inside of me."

After I cleaned my new big girl room, which was on the front left part of the house when facing the street and actually pretty near to the front door, I crossed the hallway to the living room where Donnie was sitting. What I did next is crucially important to both the story and the place where I've carried the guilt from these events:

I told Donnie that it was too hot to wear underwear under my jammies, which were already shorts.

"Can you tell my mom? Just so she doesn't yell when she gets home?" I asked.

Donnie looked up at me from the TV. He was smoking and drinking.

"Yeah, whatever," he said.

"Because I don't want to get in trouble anymore," I said.

"That's good," he agreed. "Maybe you can be a good girl now."

I emphatically agreed and went to bed, and he went back to his show. I thought we were talking about the new big kid room. I thought we were talking about me having my own room away from the babies.

I remember it moment by moment because what happened next stayed in my memory forever:

I woke up to his fingers inside me.

I didn't hear him enter my room.

I didn't see him moving through the darkness toward me.

I didn't hear his hot, wet breath coming toward my bed.

I hadn't realized that the objects normally scattered around my room would have at least alerted me to his presence.

---

11 Grooming: "manipulative behaviors that the abuser uses to gain access to a potential victim, coerce them to agree to the abuse, and reduce the risk of being caught."
Definition from: https://www.rainn.org/news/grooming-know-warning-signs.

12 Incidentally, it seems to be the same duality that I described earlier, where victims have to be participating in their own abuse for average people to sleep at night.

I didn't know the new room.

I tried to get away from his fingers. I tried to pretend I was pushing him off in my sleep so as not to anger him. I remember calculating that my best bet was to roll over and pull a cheap pink stuffed animal closer to my body. Just to make him stop. But not anger him.

It didn't work.

"I know you're awake, baby,"[13] he whispered.

I've blocked out the rest of that first night.

But I did try to tell my mother what was happening to me at night when she left for work.

I remember her being in the living room, standing on a step stool changing the lightbulb in an old, ornate light fixture in the middle of the room. I remember talking myself up to go tell her.

She was pregnant, I'd reasoned, and on a step stool, so how fast could she really get me if she took it badly? I approached her slowly. It didn't help. She didn't care.

More than that, she was furious with me for my "lies." She was pregnant with *his child* and she told me I was jealous of the new baby. My mother saw me at age four as competition for his sexual attention. *Her* sexual attention. The thing she used to keep *her* safe. She slapped me so hard that my head hit the floor and damaged the vision in my left eye permanently.

My mother is still alive. In my twenties, I decided to try to reconnect with her via Facebook. I thought maybe I needed closure. I wanted her to take responsibility for what she had done to me. I wanted her to tell me why. But she couldn't. She's stayed stuck at the time she started drinking and has never grown out of her teenage self. And like *all* abusers, she remembers she was a "perfect young mother" who was just taking seizure medication with alcohol. I remember her as being pregnant with my youngest brother, who wasn't born with any of the birth defects my middle brother *was* born with. Sometimes if narcissists think you don't matter, which is usually, they don't even bother to

---

13 I've never let anyone call me "baby" since. Not ever.

tell you believable lies. Also, as I've described, she was a gleeful participant in Donnie's abuse, and it definitely wasn't because of alcohol. It just made her feel good to hurt me. An inconvenient truth now, to be sure.

My mother's sister never knew we'd been permanently removed. Just to give you some scope on the denial. She'd told her sister *I had lied* about Donnie and gotten them all in trouble, but basically that we'd been removed as some sort of Hispanic DCFS quota.

People *often* ask me what it would take for me to forgive my mother. I don't know why they care. People are curious. Forgiveness is a big deal for them. What I tell people who ask is *nothing*. This isn't to say there isn't anything I would want or need to hear from a mother, things that could be very therapeutic and valuable for me to hear; what I mean is: she is who she is and she isn't capable of the type of self-awareness that would be required to come up with something worthwhile that would have meaning to me. What could she say? Nothing. There is nothing she could conceivably say to bring me to forgive her for her *crimes*. For her betrayal. And she *never* will. She once messaged me on Facebook and the opener was "Well, sorry for ruining your life, I guess." I still have it. I was so dumbfounded by what I actually received as an apology after all those years, I kept it.

Eight words: *Well, sorry for ruining your life, I guess.*

So, no, there's nothing she *could* say. Humans are socialized to believe a mother is the pinnacle of womanhood and benevolence. But I'll tell you the truth: sometimes we look for a mother and only find an abuser. A mother is more than that, and I needed to stop seeking to give her that unconditional love that I would never receive from her. I don't care what societal pressure suggests. Like my love and devotion could change her. It never did. And never has.

Like many children who are being sexually abused, I stopped prompting my mother to bathe me. I was afraid that if I ever was caught in the bathroom, Donnie would take his chance. Donnie noticed I wasn't getting clean anymore, became enraged, and convinced my human mother to buy me a douche and use it on me. With no questions. And she did. I vividly remember her sitting me on the toilet *while he instructed her on how to clean my baby bits.*

There's no way she didn't know, and that's exactly what she claims. She wasn't drugged on epilepsy medication. *She was helping him sexually abuse her daughter and now she's struggling to live with it.*

When I came into my twenties and started looking back on my memories of my mother at the time, I was a lot more forgiving:

Maybe it was the drugs. Maybe it was the seizure medication. Maybe she was too young to have kids.

She told me once that when I had my own kids, I'd understand. Don't they always say that? No doubt kids are hard, and I didn't know *how* hard. But that excuse ignores her agency. Now that I'm a mother, I *do* see it differently:

Maybe she was complicit.

My mother's favorite place to eat used to be called the Ground Round, an American casual restaurant that was pretty popular in the 1980s and 1990s. Now it's called the 99, a similar American casual restaurant like the ones you can find in most suburban areas of the country. *Totally* a different place; still her favorite. People are creatures of habit.

The Ground Round used to have this "Pay What You Weigh" deal on for kids' meals in the early nineties. There was a giant carnival-sized scale at the front of the restaurant. When kids came in, one of the first things the server did was weigh them. I weighed thirty pounds. Which means it cost them thirty cents to feed me. Donnie complained at every single pound I put on. I remember it.

"We must be feeding you too much," he'd sneer in front of the waitresses, and they'd laugh along. Because what else do people do in that situation? But, in reality, it made me think everyone was in on how he was treating me. That I deserved it. He made it seem like everyone was his friend and there was no one to tell. All abusers do this to some extent, but the practiced narcissists are especially adept. I didn't just think that either. He said it. Over and over again:

There's no one to tell.

The preschool noticed I wasn't gaining weight and appeared to be suffering from malnutrition. I was given pamphlets on childhood nutrition to take home for my mother. She threw them away and buried them in the trash so Donnie wouldn't see.

In the context of adulthood, I have a four-year-old daughter. She currently weighs forty pounds and she is quite tiny, so this would not have been an easily ignorable fact. Ten pounds off would be a quarter of her weight. Thriving is a huge part of my personality. Plus rainbows. This was noticeable. People knew.

One day, as I rode the bus I thought was taking me to the YMCA after-school program, the bus took an unexpected turn toward Donnie's house. I remember being excited.

"Look," I said to the other kids, "we're going to drive right by my house!"

The bus stopped directly outside of my house, where my mother stood, scarlet-faced and seething.

Waiting for me.

I ducked down so she wouldn't see me. Maybe the bus driver would forget I was there.

"Come on, honey, your mother is waiting for you," the bus driver called.

Aware that everyone was watching, and that my mother had absolutely no human dignity—and thus cared not a lick for mine—I walked into the onslaught of abuse I was sure would befall me the second I was outside of the sight of others.

And so it went.

Things got a lot more complicated for me after the school got involved. It turned out I had been sent home with ringworm on the inside skin of both thighs. It had been spotted when I sat down crisscross applesauce with shorts on during circle time.

I was taken to the nurse immediately.

"Well, do you ride horses??" she asked.

"I've never seen a *real* horse," I said. "I fell off an elephant one time."

Because I was four and had ADHD.

"You fell off an elephant?! When?!" she asked.

"At the circus. They put me on the back and I was too small for the rope. I fell off and they all yelled at me. But that was a long time ago. Do you mean that?"

"What? No. The circus was last year. Do you have a cat?" she asked.

"No. We can't have pets. They aren't allowed at Donnie's," I told her.

It seems the adults in my life had fast-tracked an investigation into how a malnourished child in poverty gets ringworm on her inner thighs.

Finally, it was my mean day care lady, Barbara, who got it out of me. She could always tell when I was lying, and she kind of didn't like me. I had once gotten my finger stuck in her favorite plastic lawn chair and the fire department had to come and cut me out of it. She was every strict grandmother.

She was also asking us questions and recording our responses on a tape recorder as part of some research I was never made aware of or consented to. But she never hurt me. Not like my own mother. Not like Donnie.

And she had been right.

They were *all* right. I was being sexually abused. I wasn't cleaning myself because I was being sexually abused. I fell asleep during the day in school because I was being sexually abused at night and had to stay vigilant.

I was immediately brought to an emergency therapy session with a child sexual abuse and trauma expert. My brother was brought in, too, and waited in a separate office eating McDonald's. He had been with me at day care. Kyle was still home with our mother.

It went on well into the night because Ted fell asleep on a couch, and I sat with the therapist and his terrible anatomically correct dolls.

"Where did he touch you?" he asked. "Point on the doll."

If you don't know, one of the even more distressing things that came out of necessity of children and other nonverbal people being sexually abused by adults are these dolls. They're anatomically correct, comically so in fact, and usually the man ones come with pedo 'staches, in my extensive experience. They also have pubic hair. They're horrifying. You don't want to know what they look like. It's a lot. And it's an enormous gap to close for a four-year-old sexual abuse victim when the expert is also a man. Just something to consider.

As I look back, what I remember the most about the experience was the pain of it. Not from shame, or guilt like you'd expect as an adult, but more like my whole body was on fire and every joint burned as if it were being pulled apart by forces running away from each other.

I have ADHD. The need to escape overwhelmed me on the inside, but on the outside, I chattered more about my obsessive hobbies and knowledge webs and paced the room.

Over and over the therapist asked me what had been happening, and over and over when I stoically repeated it, they weren't sure what to make of me. I didn't seem to be shy of adults. The opposite. I didn't seem to be hindered intellectually by what I was experiencing; I was ahead at preschool and could already read.

We spent the night there, and the next day Ted and I were separated. He went back home while I was placed in a nearby emergency foster home. Very nearby.

My first ever foster home was at the top of Mason Street on the right side. It was blue. It was owned by my friend and neighbor Alice's parents. She had red hair and freckles. Her parents took me in those first couple of nights, but we had to stay inside the entire time so Donnie didn't find out where I was. It was terrifying. I was worried he would sneak in the windows. Everyone agreed I couldn't stay, but Alice's mom was heartbroken to let me go into the foster care system. She gave me a tiny gold cross to wear around my neck as she wept.

"Now, don't take this off, and remember we are right here and we love you so much."

I was scared to death. I cried and begged to stay. I said I could stay inside with her forever. I couldn't even imagine what she knew about where I was going that would have warranted that intense of a reaction from her, a safe adult.

But she wasn't wrong.

Eventually, I was brought back to Donnie's home and to my mother. DCFS was still investigating, and I was happy to be with my brothers but more scared than ever. I knew I could be taken away from them and what waited for me if I was. Donnie reminded me how easy it would be for him to throw my mother and brothers out if I told on him again.

Fight or Flight

My mother was the woman who taught me that narcissistic women like to start fights between two men when they don't have any *real* power unto themselves. My mother and father had separated after we were evicted from our apartment. He got into a cycle of homelessness and drug abuse that left him unable to help us or be a parent, and we hardly ever saw him as a result. For reference, my father looks like Eddie from *Stranger Things* at this point. If Eddie had a wispy mustache and darker coloring, they'd be twinning. He still listens to Iron Maiden. It's a whole thing, so I'm going to call him Eddie.

So, when I was still living with Donnie, my father found out that Donnie had been sexually abusing me. He lost his mind. Literally. They had to put him away for a while. Of course, my mother told me it was my fault "for telling."

When Eddie got out, he went *directly* to Donnie's house and got wild. I saw the whole thing. They were rolling around in the hallway in front of the door while I was standing there terrified Donnie would kill the only parent who loved me, and I would be alone in the world.

My mother called the police and then put on her sharpest heels so she could go kick my father in the face with them. That's 100 percent what she did. I remember thinking stilettos were weapons for a lot of my childhood.

When the police got there, they arrested my father, of course, and Donnie and Kate were left to go on their merry way.

I specifically remember trying to speak to the police. I remember trying to treat them nicely so they wouldn't take my dad. The contempt these two white officers looked down at me with is a memory I'll not soon forget. It let me know I was beneath the dignity they afforded to children. Machado's bastard daughter.

The second time I met the police was when Donnie decided he was done with Kate's "cheating" and threw us out. He called the police to help all of us leave because she was hysterical. When they came to the door, I was so scared by her fear, I loudly declared that I had not told on him.

As I reflect on his comfort at calling the police, I'm still a little stunned. He knew exactly how to spin the story to these officers. That told me something important. The police are not here to protect *you*; they are here to protect *him*. Your abuser. Something about Donnie that neither I nor Kate nor my father, Eddie, had afforded him a respect we were not granted.

If you think I'm wrong, would *you* have missed a four-year-old girl loudly crying that she hadn't told on him? Probably not, right? Yeah, me neither.

In my extensive experience, your first interaction with law enforcement will basically set you up for how you feel about law enforcement for the remainder of your life. It is your frame of reference. Your lens. And people deal with that in their own ways. For example, my first interactions with the police were as the Hispanic girl, the child of a disempowered woman and a father who had a long history of arrests, drug use, and homelessness.

If your first meeting with law enforcement was with someone you knew, you're going to be more trusting. But I can see monsters, and they don't like to be seen. They like to be feared. Now, I personally know good people who are in law enforcement. But I have run into a lot of bad law enforcement. It's statistics. I was more likely to run into more law enforcement, so I know about the broader range of people *it attracts*. Law enforcement has the highest rate of domestic violence of any occupation. If you ask a nurse which occupation sends their partners to the ER most, they'll tell you. If you've never had that conversation with a nurse in your life, I invite you to ask. I think that's a fair statement. So anytime throughout this story where I talk about places where I had a bad brush with law enforcement as the victim, I acknowledge all of those things are true at once.

Also I acknowledge the system is intentionally unequal and kept so by monetary interests but that there are somehow still good people involved who are trying to make things better at every level. Burning themselves out at every level. I know and love these people. But I was not saved by them.

What more could they have done with what they had?

I probably seemed like I could fight for myself. I probably seemed like I could mother whatever children my mother chose to have for whatever reasons she chose to have them. I guess that's a stereotype I might have fit. From their lens.

As with many transitions in my childhood, out of seemingly nowhere, our entire family moved in with a guy she was cheating with, Bud. He lived at his sister's house, so we all moved in there—the three of us stuffed in a room with Bud's nine-year-old niece. A three-bedroom apartment.

Kate and Bud had sex in front of us many times. I remember one of the times. *Pet Sematary* was on. Seeing them have sex was confusing for me because I didn't realize at the time that it was so taboo, because of all the abuse I had experienced. And, with my ADHD, this would have been another place I wouldn't have recognized a social boundary that wasn't spoken aloud. So I brought it up in front of Bud's sister, and people were horrified. Actually, Bud's brother-in-law was a decent guy, as I recall, and he could hardly keep a straight face from laughing.

Kind of feels like everyone should've taken everything a little more seriously, but that's how it went.

Eventually, Bud put his hands on Kate, and she decided that meant he was no better than Donnie to her, so she made me start sleeping with scissors beneath my pillow in case he, too, tried to rape me in the night. That's what she told me would likely happen. *It had happened to her.* She told me he would rape and murder me, and everyone else in the room, if I didn't keep the scissors. I still remember the pillowcase under which I kept those scissors. I'll never forget the yellow flowers on the fabric hiding the scissors that would protect me from rape and murder.

Of course, I didn't sleep at all. I just watched my brothers all night, clutching my scissors. I was probably five by then so that would make her twenty-four.

One night, Kate decided to make her escape from Bud. She didn't tell me where we were going or anything about it. It was just time to get out. Again.

She packed all of our stuff into a black trash bag and threw it in the back of her car with the two boys. As she and I were making our final escape, Bud woke up, wise to us leaving.

"Hurry up," I said to her.

"Kate?!" he shouted.

I stopped to listen, and in the dark, I met her eyes and they were wide like I'd never seen them.

She let out a shriek, shouted, "Run!" and bolted for the car, leaving me behind with the bags.

I dropped everything in my arms and ran as fast as I could to the passenger car door while he chased her to the driver's door. I remember the door was almost too heavy for me to pull open. She had one of those old eighties cars that had two doors where you had to pull the front seat up to let people in the back.

I remember how fast he looked. I remember him jumping over the tiny hill that felt like a mountain when I climbed it. He ran to her door first, but she'd locked it and pressed her back against her door. He then ran around to my side while I screamed and prayed that the door was all the way shut so it would latch and could lock.

It was.

By some miracle, I mustered the strength to heave that huge door shut hard enough to save us all. No thanks to her, of course.

She'd left me to die. Literally.

Bud started beating on my door with his fist.

"Open the door, you little b——h, or I'll kill you!" he screamed at me.

I believed him. I backed all the way up to my mother.

"No! Please no!" I screamed back.

The boys were scream-crying in the back seat.

If you've never heard the shriek of a baby or child who's survival-crying, afraid for their life, it is absolutely awful. They can't breathe but need to wail in alarm. I'll never forget the screams of my baby brothers as Bud raged and promised to kill us all.

My mother sat there just watching him.

"DRIVE!" I screamed at her.

But she just watched, seeming to consider his rage. Enjoying my fear, maybe. It felt like forever, but it was probably only moments.

"Fine," she finally said.

She turned the keys and the car turned over.

Bud roared with rage.

"B——H! You aren't f———g leaving me, you f———g b——h! I'll kill you. I'm going to rape your daughter! I'm going to bury you with your f———g kids, you f———g b——h!"

Kate pulled away.

I never saw Bud again, and Kate and I never talked about the incident again.

But I still live in the city in which it happened, and I still drive by that apartment building every once in a while. Every time, I wonder whether he ever found another woman with kids to hurt.

The apartment building is a seafoam green now, the only one that color in town, but somehow even that doesn't make it less ominous to me.

We had a social worker checking on us by this point, given the extensive history of abuse. So, of course, DCFS came for us after that, and it was permanent.

Those were my last days living with Kate.

But I learned a lot about this world by being small in it.

Bastard doesn't just mean your parents weren't married. Sometimes it means the adults around can't consider you a *real* child because they need to make you at fault for your own abuse. For any number of reasons. But, in my experience, it's because they're the ones doing the harm. Or needing to ignore it on your behalf.

"Let me give you some counsel, bastard. Never forget what you are, for surely the world will not. Make it your strength. Then it can never be your weakness. Armor yourself in it, and it will never be used to hurt you."[14]

---

14 George R. R. Martin, *A Game of Thrones* (New York: Bantam Books, 1996).

Sesame Street

I watched a documentary recently on HBO called *Street Gang: How We Got To Sesame Street*[15] about how and why the show *Sesame Street* was developed. It turns out, the show's creators, including Jim Henson and Joan Ganz Cooney, wanted to see whether they could use the television kids were already watching to reach and teach them.

The show's target market was kids like me and others going through similar or adjacent poverty situations. Latchkey kids. They saw me. And I saw them.

When people ask me what I think impacted me the most in my origin story to become this—whatever "this" is—I always say "reading." And I specifically credit *Sesame Street*, *Mister Rogers' Neighborhood*, and LeVar Burton of *Reading Rainbow*, along with all of those teams, with inspiring me to read and teaching me what I needed to learn to become a functional human being.

So, if you're going anecdotally by me, PBS is love and I will always be a supporter. My love of reading inspired a love of learning, which inspired a love of ideas, history, people, music, science, and all the things that would touch my life and help me remain alive today.

---

15   *Street Gang: How We Got to Sesame Street*, directed my Marilyn Agrelo (New York: Screen Media, 2021), https://streetgangmovie.com/, accessed 31 May 2022.

But I didn't just inherently know I had value as a child in the world. I had value because people who really cared about the world saw me and took the time to reach out across the screen and teach me that.

I'm here because Fred Rogers told me it was okay to have big feelings and that he liked me just the way I was. I'm here because LeVar Burton told me *not to just take his word for it.*

I'm here and thriving because of people who were in the same world and chose to make it better, rather than make it worse.

If I am anything, it is because I had someone else's shoulders to stand on. Because I had a safe harbor to learn to read in.

It mattered.

Thank you, PBS.

Trash

They don't keep you together when you get taken away from your family. They usually can't. The foster care system is entirely overburdened; it has no extra resources, and there are currently about half a million American children in care nationally on any given day. Those numbers have been exacerbated by the COVID-19 pandemic and the opioid epidemic.

The foster care system is one of those things that "just happens" to kids. But people don't like things that can "just happen" to people because that's scary. If it can happen to anyone, then it can happen to them. So instead, we look for the Bad Actor.[16] The thing that makes this your fault, even if we can't say that out loud. In reality, what has happened is that systemic oppression is real, it didn't "just happen" to families, but we don't like to examine the root causes.

So, in my experience, people need to think that kids who end up in foster care have some part that they played in their own tragic circumstances. It's the Quiet Part.[17] The understood part. The coded language part. Trust me, I know a lot about coded language. And I don't blame people for blaming me

---

16 **The Bad Actor**: the person who has taken an action to make a bad thing happen—either to themselves or someone else.

17 **The Quiet Part**: This is the part of a conversation either interpersonally or societally that is "understood" by participants in the discussion. These "understood" parts are usually too terrible to say out loud and usually go largely unexamined but commonly repeated as a result.

for where I found myself. If people didn't think I was responsible for the terrible situation I found myself in, how could they say they care about children as humans? How could they sleep at night knowing how many more children are being placed in care now than ever before? When situations and circumstances are the worst they've been in generations? How could they continue to make laws against the LGBTQ+ community if they knew how involved they are statistically in helping raise these "throwaway kids"? Because so many were thrown away themselves.

There's actually been science around this, horrifyingly enough. So many people sent this to me, so I feel compelled to share it with you. In Germany, then (currently?) renowned sexologist, and *admitted* pedophile Helmut Kentler started a social experiment with influential men who were pedophiles (**not gay**) by placing foster children in their care and "seeing what would happen."[18] When I read the article about it in the *New Yorker*, the thing that struck me was *how many of Kentler's colleagues knew* what was going on. Indeed, the thing that seems to have been the easiest part was convincing other adults that some people's children were just second-class children unworthy of concern or protection. Kentler wasn't gay; he was a pedophile. There's a significant difference there that, apparently only after the death of his own adopted son by suicide due to abuse, *Kentler himself acknowledged.*

So, when you're watching *Criminal Minds* or some other crime procedural and hear the actors say, "He bounced around in foster care," as a well-known stop on the Future Serial Killer Path, that harms me. It makes me feel like an alien. Like I was responsible for this.

I wasn't. I was just born. Like you. Except you were born to your family, and I was born to abusers. Or maybe we were both born to abusers. There are a lot of kinds of abuse. Neglect is abuse too; it's actually the most common form of child abuse.

---

18   Rachel Aviv, "The German Experiment That Placed Foster Children with Pedophiles," *New Yorker*, July 19, 2021, https://www.newyorker.com/magazine/2021/07/26/the-german-experiment-that-placed-foster-children-with-pedophiles.

I find this same phenomenon around domestic violence; we blame the victim rather than the Bad Actor. A woman gets beaten by her husband every day until one day he kills her.

Why didn't she leave him?

A woman gets raped, we blame her for it.

Well, what was she wearing? How much had she had to drink? Where was she?

We think by doing so we can separate ourselves from the victim of things that "just happen." This way we can stop bad things from happening to us by wrongly believing, even if it's just a little bit, that these victims were at least partly to blame for their sad circumstances. You know what people don't see? The Quiet Part.

If you are neurodiverse like I am, you may often miss the Quiet Part because it is usually an unspoken phenomenon understood by all members of a conversation. It's a dirty secret no one wants to acknowledge but everyone fully understands. Like a pedophile uncle people keep their kids away from but never exile from family gatherings.

Or those "*Where was she?*" whispers in response to attacks against women, as if there are places women can't exist without expecting to be raped or killed. That's pretty loud for the neurodiverse.

Or the "*What was she wearing?*" whispers, as if there are things a woman can't wear if she doesn't want to be attacked or killed.

Or, in the case of my childhood abuse, "*I'm sure she deserves it.*"

I've watched so many adults in my life turn a blind eye to obvious physical child abuse under exactly this premise.

So, to follow that logic, what is the Quiet Part in witnessing child abuse and thinking or even agreeing with the child's abuser that "I'm sure she deserves it"?

That there are children who are less worthy of the protection we would afford to our own children. Even at their worst.

And if we look at the state of foster care in America, we can clearly see that that is the truth.

There are children we care about *less*. Who matter *less*.

But they aren't any less of a child, so they don't understand why they're being rejected.

That was a loud lesson.

Ted and I were in foster care together. Kyle was taken separately. He got put in nicer foster homes because people like to take care of babies, and DCFS prioritizes those relationships for obvious emergency reasons; namely, they need to go back to them a lot. Kyle went to this lovely woman, Dana, and her family in the very nice area of town in which I live now.

When I was six and Ted was five, we were placed in a foster home that was a double-wide trailer in the town next door.

My memory of the Trailer is you'd walk into a living room that had a kitchen in it and you'd walk past a kitchen on your right and go back to a three-bedroom trailer. The foster kids slept in one room, "the Foster Kid Bedroom"; the parents slept in a room; and Luke, their evil seventeen-year-old son, had his own room. They had to lock him in his room at night so he didn't hurt the other kids.

Can you imagine putting abused kids in that situation? No? Me neither. Yet that was the reality for Ted and me.

The first night, Monica, the eldest foster care daughter, was showing me the Foster Kid Bedroom when I noticed one of the little girls changing fully naked in the hallway. Her braids hung down by her ears like my Pippy Longstocking doll.

"What is she doing?" I asked Monica.

"What? Oh her? That's Rocky, the reta——ed Indian[19] that lives here. She won't change in her room because she's scared. That's how they got her last time."

This girl is Hispanic, I thought. But I said, "How did they *get* her?"

"She was changing in her room, and then her brother and father raped her. And now she doesn't talk or wash anymore," Monica told me flatly.

---

19 Apologies for the ableist term, and the gross racism; it's a quote. As you have and will see from other quotes, I've taken care to remove enough of the curses, ableist terms, and racist slurs from the quotes in this book so you know what was said without having to experience the exact conversations I did as a child. It's important for the story to fully understand, I believe, however, so I include enough for you to make the connection.

"How do you know she's an Indian if she can't talk?" I asked.

"The braids?" Monica said, like I'd missed something obvious.

The what?!

"You should ask her!" Luke the evil brother chimed in, tapping his finger on the little girl's head. "But she won't answer you because they raped her brain out! Didn't they, Injun[20]?" he sang out gleefully.

The sad little girl looked right through him.

This is so bad.

I followed Monica into the Foster Kid Bedroom, which had two sets of bunk beds, each of which slept two kids per bed. Seriously.

"I need to sleep with my brother," I told her.

"No," Monica said. "The boys sleep on that bunk and the girls sleep on that bunk." She pointed to each bed.

"Well, Ted isn't potty-trained yet, and I'll need to change him if we're all going to stay in a room together," I said.

"Well, I'm sure we can work that out then," Monica said.

"But first, this is the Closet," she said, indicating to the paneling we were standing in front of.

She knocked. No one answered.

"Always knock," she warned me.

I nodded solemnly.

"And now we go in," she said.

She went into the closet and pulled me in.

"Wow! Cool closet," I said.

And then I noticed Monica taking off her clothes.

"Is this where we change for privacy instead?" I asked her.

"No," she scoffed.

"Should I take my clothes off too?" I asked.

"Why would you do that?" she asked.

"Because you're taking yours off?" I whispered.

---

20 Apologies for quoting this slur. Not much I can do to adjust this word. Can you imagine Rocky hearing this repeatedly, especially after everything they did to her?

After her clothes were off, she sat down and spread open her legs.

"Now," she said matter-of-factly, "I can protect you from Luke, but he'll hurt me too, so you're going to need to make it worth it for me."

I stared at her, considering what she was asking me.

This is so bad.

"Why wouldn't I just tell?" I asked.

"Because if you do, I'll *give you* to Luke," she said.

"You want to be Luke's toy or my friend? Because Rocky used to talk before Luke got her."

The idea of being locked in my mind the way Rocky seemed to be scared me more than Monica did. More than anything. To this day.

"What about my brother?" I asked.

"You can protect your brother and I can protect you," she said.

"Okay," I said.

"See, they told me you were smart," she said.

And that was how I found out that sexual abusers can be women. Monica shared a bedroom with me for a full year. And still, as I look back, Luke was the truly evil one. I know. I hear it too. But, seriously. An evil partnership.

One of the times the foster parents went out to dinner, they left us all in the care of Monica and Luke who then decided for entertainment they would show us all how they sexually abused the toddler who was living there. Who was in a diaper. He was also Hispanic.

I don't recall the foster parents ever doing anything harmful to any of us, but they did keep those two kids full up with victims, and it wasn't like they didn't know. *They locked his bedroom at night.*

They knew what was happening.

They just didn't care.

Once, I was sick, and the foster mother, Carly, asked me to come into her room so she could check my temperature. Luke, her psychotic son, was curled up on his mother's bed always needing to be the center of her attention. I was facing her, getting my temperature taken, and my hand was on her bed while I waited, too near to his mother to Luke's liking, so he silently bent my finger back trying to get me to move it away from the pain. Away from *her*. I looked right into his face and dared him to hurt me in front of his mother.

At first, he was surprised. Then angry. Then a slow smile crept to his face.

"Where's your idiot little brother right now?" he asked. "I think I'd like to play with him."

"Luke!" his mom cried. "Don't say 'idiot.' He's handicapped because her mother drank with him!"

As if I wasn't standing there.

"If I had her as a daughter, I'd drink too," Luke responded.

I felt my face burn from the heat of shame, but I didn't know why.

"Luke!" Carly shouted.

"What? You're telling me she's a good kid? You know how many family members she probably has, *and none of them want her?!*"

"Well, they *do* have big families," she agreed.

"Get out of here, Sp—c!"[21] he sneered.

I ran into the Foster Kid Bedroom and cried. I didn't know what he had called me, but I knew it wasn't good. And something about everything that happened was my fault.

Maybe it was why I didn't matter and people had left me here.

Ted and I went to school nearby at the closest public elementary school. The bus would pick us up at the top of the street, which was a major highway, and drop us off early at the gym. The gym led to the cafeteria, which was where they served their free breakfast program.

When we'd walk in, the principal would greet us at the door. Rubbing his hands together, he'd say:

"Good morning, students! Let's get breakfast; let's pick some good food to nourish our bodies so we can fill our brains and learn and make good choices."

We still always picked Fruit Loops with milk, but I remember being grateful to him for normalizing what was a very shame-filled activity: getting free food from school. I actually never got used to that. I would feel shame about

---

21   Apologies again for a slur.

it every day until we stopped being eligible in middle school. Then I just went hungry. But let's be real: you're supposed to. You're supposed to feel shame. Shame and groveling gratitude. Look at how they talk about social programs *now*. It wasn't like they were more inclusive *before*.

One day, the school hosted a Grandparents' Day, where everyone was to invite their grandparents and we'd show off all the things we were learning to them. I wasn't allowed to invite my grandparents for safety reasons because your family isn't allowed to know where you are in foster care. I wasn't even allowed access to a phone.

When everyone else's grandparents came, I sat in the corner alone reading to myself. I was reading my favorite book, *Cloudy with a Chance of Meatballs*, which was about food falling from the sky and everyone always having plenty to eat.

I had my hair in pigtails and I was wearing blue overalls that day. As I read, an older man approached me and smiled kindly. He was tall, balding, with blue eyes and white hair. He had a white mustache. He asked whether I wanted to read my book to him. I did. We sat together quietly reading in the corner, and a reporter from the local paper came by and took our picture. My grandmother kept the picture on her fridge.

When the reporter asked who he was, he said he was my grandfather. Here's where I get a little unsure this man wasn't an actual angel: he was also the custodian at one of my first "foster" schools. I called him "Mr. S."[22]

We were finally removed from the Trailer when it got shut down. Apparently, one of the verbal kids had managed to relay what was happening to a social worker who was paying attention, and it was so egregious when the full story came out that it made the news. I know that because I was living with a narcissist at the time, and she saw the article and crowed to everyone she knew about how I had lived there for over a year.

---

22 Unlike with other people in this book, now that I actually reflect on Mr. S, I hope people who know me and my story know who I'm talking about when I mention Mr. S. Or maybe that's just some life magic. I'll never know. But I'm grateful. With the others, I would much rather you and others focus on what happened, what continues to happen, and what we can all do to help. But, with Mr. S, I hope everyone knows how special he was.

I ran into Luke again at a nearby mall one day when I was around eight. Almost two years later. He looked right at me and sneered. I was frozen to the ground. My whole body just shut down. He seemed even more delighted by my response, so I must have looked really afraid. He put his finger to his lips, said, "Shhh," and then walked away with his friend, never looking back at me.

I threw up right where I was standing. My foster mother flipped out at me and told me I needed to clean it up while a store attendant rushed over and tried to minimize what was happening. I didn't hear anything they said. The store attendant was nice, but I got beaten when I got home anyway.

I never saw Luke again. Still living so close to the Trailer, sometimes I think I see him places when I go too close to that area. But it's never him. I never went back to that store, though. Luke can have it.

Years later, as I thought back to what was going on then, I tried to find the article about the Trailer again. All I found was a story about another kid who was about my age and was in jail for abusing his own children. The story said he felt like he never had a chance because he'd been placed in that kind of home and just never got any help. I felt sick. I wondered whether he was the baby Luke and Monica had been abusing. I wondered why I'm different. I wondered whether I was broken. I wondered whether the evil that was poured into me would someday manifest me into some monster too. The monster I could see crouching in others; barely hidden by their people-mask. *The ones who blamed the world for them becoming abusers too.*

But my monster never came.

The Evil You Know

A round 1991, when I was about seven years old, we were brought to the last foster home I'd live in.

Ted, my middle brother, and I were still together, and there was only one other foster child in the home, Becky, plus the family's biological children: a newborn named Chavonne and a teenage son, Neil.

The house was a ranch and had an above-ground swimming pool. The family was barely working middle class, when that was a thing, but seemed filthy rich in my mind.

I still missed my youngest brother, Kyle, but they told me I couldn't see him because he was living with my mother at the time and she still had some work to do. I was heartbroken to not see him. How could it be safe for him to live there, but not safe for me to see him?

"Her boyfriends," the social workers and the foster mother would all agree. "Do you want to meet any more of her boyfriends?"

I did not.

We used to go on supervised visits to see her, and she would sometimes come to play games with us in a room at the Massachusetts Society for the Prevention of Cruelty to Children (MSPCC)[23] offices. Then one day, with no

---

23   The Massachusetts Society for the Prevention of Cruelty to Children, which is a nongovernment organization. It's not part of DCFS, which when I was a kid was called

47

warning or reason, she stopped showing up. Our social worker would pick us up from our foster home for our visit, we'd wait for the whole scheduled time, our mother just wouldn't show up, and I would go back brokenhearted. I still needed my mother to love me. Even after all the abuse, I needed her love to validate my worthiness to be loved. But she couldn't give it.

One of the things that is most fascinating about foster kids is how desperately we cling to abusive family members. Just to feel safe. Just to feel normal. I didn't need her. I needed *a mother*. But how could I know? No one knows.

My social worker would remind us that we couldn't go back to our mother if she didn't get her act together. From what we saw, she didn't even care to visit us, so it didn't seem very likely.

Eventually, we lost hope and stopped going to visits ourselves. Ted stopped going to visits first. Karen, our foster mother, would offer him trips to the ice cream parlor or Toys"R"Us instead. I begged her to wait and take me too, but that wasn't what she wanted:

"If you felt like you were *my daughter*, you wouldn't need any other mother," she said.

Monarch of the Gaslight.

That was always Karen's way, as it is with all abusers: prove you're worthy of the place I will never give you, no matter what you do.

But I kept trying to see my biological mother. The social workers would confirm the appointments, Kate would say she'd be there, but then she'd just never show up. Each time, I'd take the thirty-minute drive to the MSPCC office, wait in the lobby, cry for the length of the agreed-upon visit, and then drive thirty minutes back. Heartbroken.

Eventually, the social workers wouldn't even drive us there anymore, and MSPCC started using a taxi service where strangers would pick us up and take us to visits, doctor's appointments, and our required therapy. Always the bare minimum of care.

"DSS" or Department of Social Services.

One of the drivers got to know us a little. I remember him as a bit of a strange man whom I was a little scared of at first. But, eventually, he got to know us and demanded to MSPCC that we schedule what we needed to do while he was working. I heard the whole conversation through his dispatcher on the radio.

I think his name *actually was* Eddie. He was Black, wore a flat cap, and used to make us laugh. His taxi smelled like clove cigarettes. He was appalled that they just let two little kids get into cabs with total strangers and would often go on long social justice impact rants. He only missed picking me up one time, when he was super sick. But he'd called and told social services to cancel our appointments that day; they just hadn't. He was the first person I can remember who made me believe in the kindness of people. He fought for my dignity. We're not in touch anymore, but I would love to thank him. He was another angel who saw what I was going through for real and helped me get by.

After another period of no-shows, social services stopped scheduling the visits with my mother. They told me she'd offered to give up her parental rights to us if they would let her keep my baby brother, Kyle, and as long as we kept our last name, Machado. I have no idea whether that's completely true, but it's what I was told at the time. I didn't know adults could lie yet. I didn't know about gaslighting and self-serving manipulation strategies.

The last foster family I was in, "the Smiths," wanted us to stay. I literally did not care what they did, and I was never going to say anything about it because I didn't want to leave. The evil you know is better than the evil you don't, especially when you know what's *really* out there like I did. At the Smiths' house, no one came into my room at night while I was sleeping, and anything short of that was survivable. If they didn't sexually abuse me, I could stay and survive. Or so I thought.

Unfortunately, after we weren't being picked up for visits every week anymore, that's when things started to change.

The Foster Mother, Karen Smith, had blond hair and blue eyes. She was about 5'4", but she seemed so much bigger in my mind. She had been prom queen and beautiful once. At least that's how she told the story. Weirdly, she'd bring it up to every new person she met and would have to meet new people a lot because she's a full-blown politician-level narcissist, so there's a lot of turnover around her.

Karen never worked or did anything else after high school other than have children and "raise them," so to speak. And shopped. She was forty-four years old when I was brought there to stay.

These days, Karen is in her late seventies and looks like the older mom from *Everyone Loves Raymond*. The hate has left its mark.

The Foster Father,[24] Willy Smith, was forty-five years old and also blond with blue eyes. He was a landscaper and ran his own business cleaning parking lots. He had been abused as a child by his mother and siblings and clearly had a lot going on. His mother had him ten years after her eldest son and carried a lot of shame around being pregnant with him, so much so that she tried to force a miscarriage by wearing too-tight garters and cinches. He repeated that story a lot.

Willy was the youngest in a "very rough" (his words) Polish immigrant family. He had dropped out of high school as a teenager to work for his father's trucking business in the mid-1960s.

When the Vietnam War draft came down, Willy married Karen when they were drafting single men. Then when they were taking married men, but not fathers, they had their first child to avoid the draft. When they told the story, they recalled it with humor; they just kept having kids to avoid the draft until the war was over, although two of his brothers went. He felt a lot of shame about that, too, which I guess is why he told the story with such self-deprecating humor.

Later, his older brother took over his father's trucking business, and Willy felt like he was forced to go out on his own, or at least that's how they tell it.

He was an alcoholic, and Karen berated him and shamed him about it, often in public and at nearly every opportunity. I really felt sorry for him more than anything.

---

24   Please see the cast list at the front of the book for clarity.

I always felt like he was never the "true" abuser and was often being manip-ulated as Karen's weapon against us as much as anything. But in the context of adult reflection, he wasn't just a weapon she used to harm us; he perpetuated his own harm.

I remember the only time I ever got spanked in my life. I was ten years old and he was taking a shower.

"Dian-er!" he yelled from the bathroom in a singsong voice. "Your mother left and didn't leave out any underwear! I don't have any in the drawer! I don't know what she does all day besides shop! Go down to the dryer and bring them up!"

I heard him. I remember exactly what he said to this day. But I was also dancing around in the living room when he said it and I forgot to get him the underwear. *I have ADHD.*

He came out in a towel, grabbed me by my hair to keep me from running, and started hitting me as hard as he could. Over and over again. He didn't say a word the entire time.

"Stop!" I begged. "I'll go right now! I forgot! I just forgot!"

His towel had fallen off in the effort, and I was completely shell-shocked by his adult male nudity. I stopped begging and waited for him to finish taking his pound of flesh.

Because let's be real; that's what was happening.

He wasn't teaching me a lesson. He wasn't helping me be a better human.

He was taking out his frustrations at many things in his life, not the least of which was that apparently he'd be left to dress himself and he wasn't used to it. So he, an adult man, naked, beat a ten-year-old rape victim with a docu-mented attention disorder like the coward with no honor he was.

"Now," he announced, physically winded, and grabbing his towel, "go downstairs, and get my underwear from the dryer."

I slid down the wall of the stairs to the basement, unable to walk on my own. Beaten viciously from my shoulders to my legs because I'd been so small.

Maybe he *was* her enabler.

But he had his own darkness for which he was responsible.

Speaking of the *darkness* abusers pass down, Willy and Karen's eldest son, Keith, was about twenty-four when I met him. He was angry at life and had red hair and freckles. Keith had married at twenty-one (she was seventeen). They had two children and an abusive marriage. Naturally.

When I was a small child, I was swimming in the deep end of a pool at a family pool party. Out of nowhere, Keith jumped in after me and held me under with his feet. I thrashed desperately for air until he must've had a change of heart and let me surface. As I gulped air and sobbed, my lungs and nose felt like they were on fire, and I was almost too weak to swim to the side. I didn't even have the strength to pull myself out, just away from him to the side of the pool. I just held onto the side and looked desperately around to see whether anyone could see me. Karen was looking down at me from her poolside chair. As I look back on it, her face seemed impassive but curious.

Almost *intrigued by what Keith might do.*

"Please," I begged her, gasping. "He tried to drown me!"

"He was just kidding!" Karen said. "Don't be so dramatic; that's why no one likes you. Is this how you act when people try to play and include you?"

Is this how you act when people try to include you? Gaslighting.

Karen went back to her conversation. I turned around to see whether Keith was behind me, and he just dead-eyed me. Not scared that I'd told someone. Not sorry he'd done it. Just totally emotionless.

Like a shark.

An important part of this story is that Karen had nearly drowned herself as a child and, as a result, was deathly afraid of water. She talked about it the whole summer long. Every summer. Every year. Karen would loudly proclaim to anyone who didn't know "that's why all my kids take swim lessons!" And people would applaud her self-awareness. Karen couldn't even take showers because she couldn't have water in her face. She had to take baths. But she was apparently just mildly interested to see whether I would drown, or, more accurately, whether Keith would drown me. Or both, perhaps. But it matters because some children matter less to some people.

Especially if those people are narcissists.

Keith ended up getting married twice. When I came on the scene, he was still with his first wife, Peggy. Peggy was barely twenty-one at the time, pretty and funny. She was kind to me and really defiant toward the Keith and Karen manipulation team. Keith was building a house for them and their two children in the town next door, about twenty minutes away, when she left him. Karen was enraged when that happened. At the time, Karen said it was because "Keith has done so much for Peggy, how dare she," but now as I think back as an adult, it seems more like when someone would leave Karen's sphere of influence, she'd do her best to *burn them down*. This is a narcissist thing.

Peggy, for example, was said to be engaged in a sexual relationship with both her father and brother. "That's why Keith left her," Karen had said about it.

Karen even wrote a letter to the Catholic archdiocese to try to get Keith and Peggy's marriage annulled. A marriage that had produced two children. Karen wanted it annulled. She wrote a thirty -page rant letter[25] to them. Well, she dictated it. I typed it. To no avail. Obviously.

When their divorce became final, Keith moved back into the finished basement of the Homestead. He was there when he met the person who would become his second, *especially* young wife,[26] Mae.

Mae was also just seventeen and had been tutoring Willy and Karen's fourth child, Neil, who was in high school with Mae, when she came into our lives. Just the perfect example of what humanity can be like. Neil caught mono and had to be out of school a lot. By the way, when he gave mono to me, I was not seen by a doctor and missed quite a bit of school, falling asleep in the library. Or at church, or when Keith made me ride with him to pick up his kids for custody agreements "as a witness." They thought I was abusing drugs at school. Only Karen knew the truth. And she could've gotten me the same resources the school system had provided for Neil, but

---

25 Long-winded "rant letters" to authorities are another hallmark of narcissism. As are winding rant phone messages.

26 I hesitate to say "child bride" here because it's a little inflammatory, but I also don't like the term "underage girl." That language is doing a lot of heavy lifting making grooming and pedophilia seem more okay, and I'm not here to perpetuate that.

over her dead body was I going to be sleeping or recovering when I could be suffering and cleaning.

There is no one who escaped Karen's influence that will tell you I'm lying.

Mae started as the tutor, then became the family babysitter, and then started dating Keith. He quietly groomed her while it was illegal, and then dated her more loudly when she was older. This is how grooming works. He was a clean ten years older than her. While it was happening, I was pretty young, probably like eleven, and Mae was about six years older than me. Mae really had her life together and thought I was smart and great, even though Karen did her best to poison her against me. I love Mae. The fact that Mae always made me feel like I was going to make it was probably a contributing factor to the life I'm living today. Mae's love showed me I had value.

As a matter of fact, Mae married my partner and me in 2015. I was thrilled she could be part of our ceremony since she had shown so much love for me in my life.

Ultimately, Mae and Keith did not stay married. Keith exhibited a lot of the same abusive behaviors his mother, Karen, had, and I would not be surprised to find out Mae was living in an abusive situation before she left him. She'd hinted, and I'd come to that conclusion because Keith hates women and was abusive toward me even when I was a teenager. He once caught me sneaking out at seventeen to meet some friends from work, and he took it upon himself to viciously beat me. Mae tried to stop him and he berated her. He called me a "sl—t" and raged that I was "sneaking out to meet a boy for sex." At seventeen. Every accusation is a confession.

In real life, one of the cool kids I waited tables with, who was a senior and captain of the football team at school, had invited all the kids he worked with to his house after work while his parents were away. He lived within walking distance. I tried to explain this during the attack, that I just wanted to fit in, but it was no use. I cried and begged him to just tell Karen, so I could explain to her, but he said, "You're not getting away with this," and twisted my arm until he fractured my wrist and three fingers.

Karen blamed the injury on sports when people asked. I'd long given up trying to explain what was actually going on with me. No one had ever believed me over Karen. And at that point? *Hardly anyone asked.*

Karen's second child was a daughter, Marie. She was twenty-three and beautiful, with blond hair and bright blue eyes. She is still gorgeous; she never ages. Marie has a daughter who is a month older than me, Jessica. Jessica and I were in school together, and we basically lived on top of each other for years. Marie was married to a police officer, and they had four children. He was pretty funny and nice to me. They later adopted two more children from foster care. Marie's children and I are still close and were basically raised together. I assume she had a hand in teaching her children that what was going on with me was not my fault because her kids were always good to me, as was she.

That marriage didn't work out, but she's remarried now and very happy. Marie went through all of the same things with the Smiths that I went through, except a generation before me, which she shared with me when I was a teenager. Realizing Karen's behavior had little, if anything, to do with me changed my entire frame of reference for what was happening. This wasn't about me; this was about Karen.

Abusive families often have kids they abuse, while others are treated like gold. In the older generation, Keith and Will, the second son, were better treated and Marie was abused by Karen, and by her own brothers to some extent. Marie's brothers took part in her abuse because Karen gave them permission.

At the Ranch, Neil, Becky, and Chavonne were treated like children, and Ted and I were treated like subhumans, in-home slaves who should be appreciative of the fact that they weren't in "the Trailer" anymore. I *was* very grateful at first, but things deteriorated when we moved from the Ranch house to the one that Karen grew up in, the Homestead. Her mother had died violently and unexpectedly in a hit-and-run accident. We moved into her mother's home because it offered more space. This had an especially deleterious impact on Karen's ability to pretend she was mentally healthy.

Five of us lived in the Homestead. There was Neil, who was fourteen when I moved in. He had red hair and blue eyes. He had been sickly as a child and

Karen "babied him," according to his older brothers. He played hockey, and I remember looking up to him to fit in. Playing hockey was a big deal in town. It still is. He was kind to me. He probably saved all our lives.

I was next, at seven years old. I was still very small for my age when I got there. I talked nonstop and asked questions incessantly. Especially since I was also a voracious reader who has an almost eidetic memory. When I read, my brain processes the information from the previous page while I read the page I'm currently on. It's great for speed-reading, but not great for pretending you're just a normal kid who isn't smarter than the adults at home. They certainly knew it. I just didn't know why they cared.

My middle brother, Ted, was next, thirteen months younger than me, age six. Also small, Ted has green eyes and brown hair. He's developmentally delayed and again, has drug and fetal alcohol syndrome. He was mostly non-verbal when we arrived. When he spoke, only I could understand his language. Because I was scared of him being beaten for it, I often told people what he said rather than letting them force him to repeat himself until he got it right.

I just couldn't make them understand that his speech issues weren't the result of him being too "lazy" to communicate clearly.

Karen shamed and beat me for translating for Ted. She told everyone I was the reason he couldn't talk. And, as I have mentioned many times now, most people don't know anyone in foster care, or certainly don't know how it really works, or, apparently, how child development works. So they *just believed her*. Or maybe they didn't, who knows? Either way, they weren't moved to stop her, so it amounted to the same thing for me.

Next in the foster family is a daughter, Becky, who is five years younger than me and was two and a half when we got there. She has olive skin, dark brown eyes, and dark brown hair. Her people come from the same place as mine, but I have much lighter coloring because my mother is Irish. Her mother was schizophrenic and thirty years younger than her father.

Becky's father had wanted a boy and regularly beat her mother, so when Becky was born a girl, her mother abandoned her at the hospital insisting she'd had a boy who died. The nurse who delivered Becky named the abandoned child *after herself*. I'm hazier on how that whole story went, but the State of Massachusetts took her away at birth and she'd been with the Smiths ever since. They were trying to adopt her, but her birth family was fighting to get her back, apparently. Becky was still doing visits with her biological parents.

Karen tried desperately to get those to stop, just as she had with Ted and me, which is just *not* the point of foster care. It wasn't supposed to be a family growing mechanism for mentally unwell abusers to find more victims.

Karen had had a few miscarriages before she and Willy got into foster care. It was Karen's only option to continue bringing children to abuse into her home. It had nothing to do with me. Or any of us. Her own children had left home, and she needed to hurt children to feel okay.

Becky developed an inability to defecate in her diaper when she was three and would attempt to hold it in. It used to get very physically distressing for her. Ever the narcissist, instead of helping the child, Karen took videos to share with others so, in her words, "they could argue in court that Becky must be being sexually abused and have her separated permanently from her parents." Or maybe Karen just said that and only took videos to share with her friends because that's what she did with them.

Becky, now thirty-four, recently took a job at the 99, (seriously, there are other restaurants here). An old family friend ran into her there recently. According to Becky, "Marie is no longer a member of the family." More than that, she tells people that "Marie is a drug-abusing drunk who cheats on her husband with strange men and is so jealous of Chavonne (the youngest) that no one in the family talks to her anymore."

When my old family friend reported this "run-in" to me, worried, asking if I'd kept in contact with Marie, I texted Marie's son to check in. I didn't want to hurt Marie's feelings by letting her know what was being said about her, apparently to literally anyone who would listen.

Marie's son was flabbergasted because *none* of what Becky said was true.

I assume that whatever Marie's newest slight against Karen was, she's really upset about it. You can tell how scared she is because of how hard she's work-ing to isolate Marie from anyone who still thinks Karen is a decent person. She has her enablers working in full-force at the lie factory. Such as they are. Karen and Marie fall out every ten years or so. Karen is supremely jealous of Marie. And she *always* has been.

Karen had adult friends who fully agreed with her behavior. Several of them. She'd be on the phone all day. Karen and her enablers would go on anti-Hispanic rants that I'd overhear. Karen was part of DCFS's foster parent directors board at one point. People who only heard who she was from her own two lips thought she was a saint.

Years later, now that I'm grown and involved in the same local organizations, I've realized that all the things Karen was saying about herself were just lies she told for her ego. Members have approached me to tell me they could prove she'd been stealing from those organizations the whole time she was involved. She wasn't prosecuted—I asked. That's the funniest part about narcissists; they always have way more to hide than you do. And, as they age, they forget what those things are and it scares them.

But I didn't forget, and neither did anyone else. A narcissist carries the seeds to their own undoing and will always be their own end.

The youngest in the family was a biological daughter, Chavonne—a "miracle baby" who was born when Karen was forty-three and Willy was forty-four. Chavonne was a toddler when I moved in and was also blond with blue eyes. I loved her a lot. She was the little sister I'd always wanted. Chavonne had a stutter when she was younger, and I taught her how to stop stuttering through love and long obsessive practice together. Just as I had for Ted. Karen would always rush Chavonne to get out what she was saying, and I would sit with her and practice, telling her I had all day. We were six years apart. Once when I was changing her shirt, she bit down on it to fight me and I pulled it out of her mouth and damaged her front tooth. I really regret that. I just had no idea it would harm the root to pull it out. I was a child. But I still regret it.

As I mentioned, Karen had had miscarriages between Neil and Chavonne, and when she was feeling particularly crazy, she'd often say I was the daughter she'd lost. She said my name would have been Jacquelyn. I felt both sad and weary at this notion. Would she have treated that daughter the way she was treating me? If Marie's abuse was anything to go by, the answer to that is most assuredly "yes."

Karen didn't let Ted or me have the same food as everyone else. We were allowed to have pasta, potatoes, and the like, boxes of fiber cereal, and basically whatever else she assigned us. Literally assigned. If we tried to eat food that wasn't ours, we could expect to catch beatings. She would leave angry and threatening messages on paper plates wedged in the cabinets when she'd leave the house.

"Do your chores! All of them! Don't touch anything in my room! The alarm is on because you can't be trusted! I know how much food there is!"

The fact that both "mothers" I'd had used food as a control mechanism really set me back well into adulthood. I have triggers about having enough food in my house. I keep "safe foods" around, still. If I don't have pasta and sauce in my house, I can't sleep. Everyone who has food triggers has their own version of that.

Our laundry was done separately, if at all, and we weren't allowed to use the same towels as everyone else. Family towels were in the towel cabinet, and our towels were to be kept in our room and could be washed with our laundry. They would always get ripped and smell, but she never changed them. She never bought us anything new. We wore hand-me-downs from different people. I got mine from Marie's daughter, Jessica, who was way taller and had a completely different body type, as well as hand-me-downs from other cousins. Ted got his from Neil and other cousins. No one ever said a thing about why we were being treated like this, and *if* they asked, it was always explained away.

"Her social worker said we have to treat her like this or she won't learn! She came to us practically feral!"

People have come to me as an adult to apologize to me because they knew what was happening—and knew it was wrong—but didn't do anything to try to help me. They didn't know how to help. It wasn't the culture at the time. Maybe you didn't interfere with other people's kids. Maybe I wasn't all the way a kid to them. I never know what to say. I'm in my late thirties now.

I don't blame those folks, not at all. But I'm an adult now. *I would know better.* And I have spent my life always asking when I see a person, especially a woman with a suspicious bruise. And I've taught my friends to always ask. I've modeled that exact behavior. Friends of mine will recount times when I specifically went out of my way to offer support to potential domestic violence victims. At college, at the bookstore, wherever. Times when I offered a hug or some sage "skillet-advice." And now they do it too. And if you know me, then that's something you can do for me now. Know better for next time, and do better when the time comes again. Don't pretend you didn't know, or that it couldn't have been happening. Don't stay wrong. Grow.

It Has to Be You

When I was eight and living with the Smiths, the State of Massachusetts finally decided to prosecute Donnie for sexual abuse.

"He's been doing this to his own daughter too," the police and investigators told me. "She's the same age as you. She's totally messed up about it and in no shape to testify. *It has to be you.* You're brave and strong. If we want to stop him from doing this to any other little girls, you need to be strong."

"Will he be there in the room?" I asked fearfully.

"Yes," they told me. "He has the right to face his accuser."

"But I don't want to 'accuse' him; I already got away," I said.

"Do you want to be responsible if some other girl gets hurt?"

I did not.

"What about your little brother? Kyle still sees his father."

I immediately agreed to be the only victim testifying in the case.

At age eight. And they *punished* me for it.

On some adult reflection as a parent, and knowing what we now know about abuse victims, it was a *seriously* low move to make me shoulder the weight of his crimes. To make the child-victim responsible for stopping him? Not the police. Not the investigators. Me. Lord, have mercy. Repeated in this weight was a lesson I'd already learned:

*Other kids are worth protecting, but you are already sullied by these crimes. So it's **your** weight to bear. Play **your** part.*

I remember being paralyzed with fear. He was going to be there, looking right at me while I told everyone what he'd done to me.

The lawyers had been very clear in my prep:

"You have to use the real words of human anatomy," they instructed.

I'd never used those words. I was afraid to tell people what he'd done to me. I felt like I had caused it. I felt like I would get in trouble too. *He told me I would.* As an adult, I still carry a shame trigger about it, even though rationally I know I had no part in the wrongdoing. I was the victim. Still, I feel shame for sharing what happened.

The trial was long and terrible. Every day I would get dressed in a Minnie Mouse (or similar) dress, tights, and patent leather shoes. My foster mother, Karen, would put my long hair up in a half ponytail and tie a bow on it. Peak narcissism. A full-on reality show for someone in her small-town life. The role of a lifetime: the Mother of the Victim.

I had to sit in the court while they chose the jury. None of the jurors looked at my face. I asked the prosecutor why.

"Don't worry," she said. "They believe you."

One by one the judge called up each potential juror and asked them whether they could put their feelings aside about the sexual assault of a child and deliver a fair and impartial verdict. Many said they could not. The judge would excuse them and they'd leave.

Even as an adult, I'll never understand that about the justice system. Anyone who thinks a baby rapist is a scum-sucking monster has to be dismissed? Who does that leave on a jury? Whose peers are those? Not mine. Then again, I've never been on a jury. I've been called three times. Every time they get one look at me and are like, "Nope. That one has strong opinions."

Fully correct. I guess you got me there.

After we got through that process, I was finally coerced into testifying. On my own behalf. On his daughter's behalf. For unknown victims who would surely come after us, without me. I say coerced because that's how it felt. Even after I had agreed to testify, every second on the stand felt like my body was wrenching and burning away from my bones.

"Why me?" I'd ask myself as I felt the shame and the pain of being revictimized the entire trial.

Karen was in High Hog Heaven. Every day her growing group of friends called her to keep her on the phone for trial updates. A lot of narcissists are emotional voyeurs, in my experience, and in a small super white suburb, there was not a lot going on. It seemed like everyone nearby knew my entire story. Maybe not everyone, but an unseemly number of moms would approach me and ask incredibly inappropriate questions at school while the trial was going on, which led to me thinking everyone knew.

This phone tree has the interesting side benefit of introducing Karen to the greater population of largely local women who would play a role in enabling her continued abuse of me.

The judge on the case "tested" my swearability at age eight.

"Much too young to be sworn in," the judge had said.

"This girl is different, Your Honor. She can do it," the state's lawyer assured the judge.

I felt proud that someone had spoken for me in this way. Also scared. *Different?* Different from what? Still a child, I didn't want to be different.

When the judge asked me whether I knew the difference between a truth and a lie, I remember parsing with her whether she meant outright lies or "white" lies, and ultimately she'd ruled I could speak for myself. At eight years old.

And I always have. No matter what it costs me.

As I made my way to the stand, the bailiff, a Black man, brought over two yellow phone books for me to sit on. I was much too small to be on the witness stand. I couldn't reach the microphone. And I couldn't see over the wall. The bailiff put one phone book down, leaned over, and whispered to me:

"Can I pick you up so I can put you on the seat? We'll just see how many books you need."

I said he could, so he lifted me up. It turned out I needed two phone books for my head to rise above the wall in front of the witness stand. I was *tiny* for my age due to stress and malnourishment.

The bailiff pushed the microphone out of the way, leaned in knowingly, and told me:

"Don't move, okay? You're balancing in a dangerous spot, and I don't want you to fall."

I nodded seriously. I *was* in a dangerous spot.

After getting sworn in, I had to tell my story . . . again . . . in front of everyone. I tried to look at only the prosecutor, but I couldn't help but look around the room. He's there. Glaring at me. With his dead, shark eyes. Whispering to his lawyer, a woman with short blond hair. They were laughing at me.

Some of the jury members were crying. *Crying.* I blamed myself. Finally, all the questions the state's lawyer had prepared me for were done. I thought that meant I was done, so I tried to slide down the books. But my bailiff friend gave me a signal that I had to wait.

The defense attorney rose and smiled at me. Not a nice smile. I can tell the difference because people with neurodiversity like mine are nearly psychic about people and vibes. Especially if they have trauma backgrounds. We're all face readers.

"We're all very sorry for what you went through," she said.

"It's okay," I answered. I had just watched some of the adult jury crying, and I was trying to minimize. Like every victim ever. I was also swinging my legs as a way of self-soothing. No one stopped me.

"Do you know what 'pretending' is?" she asked.

I told her I did. She asked me to explain what pretending is. I did my best.

She started pushing me, trying to get me to say that I was pretending that Donnie had sexually assaulted me, that I had imagined it.

"If you aren't making this up for attention, then why can't you remember everything that happened that 'first' night?" she asked.

Because I was four?

I shrugged. I didn't know and I didn't want to do it anymore. I wanted to go. I wanted to run. But I couldn't get down alone. I looked over to my bailiff friend. He had tears streaming down his face but was trying to not show it.

My awareness of his tears made me feel very afraid. I didn't understand I wasn't hurting him. I gave him a panicked look and implored him silently to take me down. He gave me a small thumbs-up.

"Didn't you mean for this to happen when you asked Donnie about your new *underwear*?" she said.

This snapped me back.

"They were new, but it was hot. That's why I asked," I answered honestly and quietly, while turning my head away to avoid Donnie's paralyzing stare.

I didn't know why she'd been asking at the time. Now I do. She was asking whether, as a four-year-old child, I was consenting to be sexually abused by asking permission to wear brand-new summer pajamas in the heat. As if a four-year-old can consent to sexual contact. *What?*

As I think back on that, I hadn't asked him about my underwear, I'd asked him about my pajamas. She deliberately misremembered it for the record. But I was eight during the trial, a much easier mark. I don't have good feelings about what kind of woman could try to trick a child into saying she consented to sexual abuse because the state had far too much evidence to get the case thrown out for her client entirely. It went to court. With a full jury. For weeks. And with an eight-year-old foster kid as a star witness.

Because I was the only one who *could* tell, and the rest of the victims weren't able.

Not because there were no other victims.

The prosecutor objected to the question and argued with the defense attorney. I got more scared than ever. Arguing adults is a trigger for children like me.

The defense attorney accused me of pretending this happened because my mother was having a new baby and I wanted more attention. I shook my head vigorously. The judge reminded me that I must answer out loud.

"No," I managed to say.

The judge told me I must speak up.

"No, I didn't!" I yelled.

The defense attorney smiled smugly, turned around, and walked back to her table where Donnie sat, also smiling.

I looked at the jury and tried to smile, too, imploring them to believe me, but no one was making eye contact. No one was even looking at me.

After the defense attorney settled into her seat, the judge told me I could get down. My new bailiff friend swooped over in three strides to take me down and walk me back to my seat. On the way, he squeezed my hand and smiled at me.

I didn't need to be there for the rest of the trial.

And when the trial ended, the jury declared Donnie "not guilty."

Karen and I went outside of the courthouse and bought flowers for the prosecuting attorney to thank her for her efforts. They sold them in the Dunkin' Donuts parking lot. When I gave them to the prosecutor, she was crying bitterly.

"They didn't believe me?" I asked her.

"No! It was my fault; they didn't believe *me*," she said as she quickly ran away from us, sobbing.

Karen said we should go. I was very distressed that the prosecutor was crying and thought I had made her cry. I had let her down. I had let all the other victims down.

As we hit the brisk air outside on the courthouse steps, I looked up at Karen:

"They didn't believe me?" I asked again, surer than before.

"No," she agreed. "They didn't."

While I was testifying, my father, Eddie, came to the courthouse. He knew I'd be there and usually couldn't know where I was. When he saw me, he pretended he'd just been there to use the bathroom and just happened to be walking by the courthouse.

I believed him because I was eight, but Karen did not. Eddie didn't care, and Karen *really* hated that. Eddie thought he was Karen's equal. She had such a thing about him and was always trying to make up lies about how he didn't love me. As an adult, I suspect that had to do with *her* father being more absent than *mine*.

A few years ago, Donnie's son, Kyle, my youngest half brother, called me. Kyle rarely calls.

"What's up?" I asked.

He was crying.

Shoot. Someone must be dead.

"I wanted to call you and let you know my dad died," he said.

My thoughts scattered.

"I'm sorry to hear that," I heard myself say. "How did he die?" I asked.

"He died in his sleep," Kyle said. "I found him. They don't suspect foul play; his window was open, so I think he died in his sleep."

I went into executive function mode.[27] We chatted a little more, I told him I was sorry for his loss, and then we hung up.

As I sat there holding my then-infant daughter, all I could feel was a flood of relief knowing we would never accidentally run into him. Knowing that every time I think I see him, I can relax in the safety of knowing it isn't actually him.

Because he died alone.

Like they all do.

Moments later, my phone alerted me that I had an email.

Sent from my birth mother to an old email address.

"Dear Di," the email read. *"Donnie has died. As you know, I expect you to be there to support your brother as a family, you can piss on his grave on your own time but right now your brother needs you to show up to his dad's funeral. Call me so we can plan."*

I just sat there. I'd seen this woman one entire time since I was removed permanently by DCFS from her care after the incident where we fled her murderous ex-boyfriend in the night. Kyle had begged me to visit Kate and have lunch at the 99 (obviously) with him. And here she was in my inbox making

---

27 ADHD-ers need to dissociate, compartmentalize, and mask our real emotions while "faking" more appropriate (more desirable?) emotions to accomplish this.

demands of me, and using the brother *she'd kept* as leverage. Not even realizing Kyle had already called me and made no such request. Hadn't even hinted at it. He knew better than to ask. Kate wanted me to show up and be paraded around as a tribute to her being a good mother in front of Donnie the baby rapist's family. Seriously. Born before shame.

I never responded to Kate's email and ultimately had to block her. She tried to get around the block with a cancer scare a few years later, but I didn't fall for that again.

Never unblock people. Trust me.

Townies

When I first came to town, I was in one of the best elementary schools. Where all the people living near the prep school sent their kids. It was in one of the nicer areas of a nice town.

I came to the school with no cohesive education. There seemed to be a plan in place to keep things to their neat little social hierarchy. For some reason, the parents were immediately informed of my presence in the school and where I had come from. They were . . . not excited. Demands were made for me to be separated from their kids, and a deal was struck where I would have to check in with the counselor.

How do I know all this? *They told me.*

This was happening alongside my court case, which was completely private but, thanks to Karen's phone tree, well publicized. It wasn't a very well-kept secret in town.

I got in trouble my first week at the new school because I'd accidentally entered the boys' lavatory. In my defense, I was wearing pants that day, and I thought the sign meant if you were wearing pants, you used that bathroom, and if you were wearing a dress, you used the dress bathroom.

Foster children are not socialized the way other children are because no adult takes them aside to explain the way things work. It's the Quiet Part again. We're just surviving day-to-day. But my lavatory mishap didn't end with just me being corrected. It went on and on. I'd followed another little boy in, so we were both pulled aside separately and asked a million different ways whether I'd followed him in to engage in sexual behavior. I was seven, or max eight. They thought because I was a victim of sexual assault, I was also a sexual predator. Which again is part of the narrative that I must be deserving of their disgust because they were "good people."

I was a child. With a processing disorder. And certainly not the person who should have borne the weight of systemic inequity, but go off, I guess.

I got bullied right away too. Bully went out of his way to point out to the other kids how poor I was, how weird I was, and how my parents hadn't wanted me. He lived nearby too. Same street. So from the second I got on the bus to the second he got off, it was nonstop.

Once during a school project on dinosaurs in first grade, I had to use ruled paper and only a pencil to color in my dino diorama because that was all I had. I'd stayed late waiting for my mother to show up for a visit, and they had no supplies there for crafts. A place where children frequently went was completely void of craft supplies. Bully walked up to me, quizzed my dino knowledge, and then called other kids over to mock me.

"Not very interesting," he said with a sneer.

They all laughed and followed him away. It was like that every single day through high school until the summer I got pretty. I tried everything. As I look back on it, knowing what I know now, it's likely every single one of those kids—especially Bully—had their parents doing their work for them. Or at least fully "helping." Did that fact ever cause them to perhaps lower their estimation of themselves in respect to me? Not once. It never even occurred to these kids that at least, unlike them, I was getting graded for work I was *actually* doing. Fascinating. Children in classrooms are often the perfect microcosm for greater society because a lot of adult people are like that too.

A lot of people who were born on third base have an easy time believing they hit a home run through hard work and dedication.

In second grade when I was first learning math, the teacher created a math competition where, each day, we would pair up and face off with a math quiz.

You could choose who you challenged. The winner's name would go on the top, and the loser's name would go on the bottom. The middling students would go in order from there. I was challenged by students every day, and I was on the bottom every day because my education to that point had not been great. I had no parents helping me at home, and the teacher was very annoyed by my presence. Like I was some repulsive thing she was forced to share air with. I had no way to learn math on my own and, every day, she announced I was the loser again for the day. Either me or the other kid who had developmental delays.

When I repeated this story on Facebook, not mentioning any names, like ten kids who were there reached out to me to tell me they remembered that story and how the teacher and her behavior had negatively impacted their lives and their relationship with education. Everyone knew who I meant.

When I was in third grade, Karen wrote a letter to my teacher and told her to stop sending me home with homework because she wasn't going to allow me to do it anymore. I had chores to do. The teacher felt sorry for me and had me stay in during recess to do my homework. She was nice. When we went on a field trip to Boston to see *The Nutcracker*, she told the students to dress up.

I didn't have anything nice to wear after I no longer needed to be paraded around court. So when I told Karen we were going into Boston for a field trip and had to dress nice, she dressed me in yellow polyester pants and a purple sweatshirt; just out of spite. I had two full-time bullies at that point, whose names I fully remember but won't reveal (more than they deserve). They were so mean to me about what Karen had dressed me in and how poor and unwanted I was. I hid in the bathroom to cry. When my teacher found me she said:

"Don't worry about those kids. The other kids like you, and you look nice."

We both knew she was lying, but it really helped to have someone to stand next to.

A lot of the parents and teachers at Best School might have treated me this way to protect the other, normal students. They felt justified. That's part of the victim-blaming narrative—the loneliness that comes from being a survivor of something like foster care.

The truth of the matter must have been too awful for them to imagine or comprehend. I hadn't done anything to deserve this. I was born into a family of drug addicts, and I bounced around in the system. And because I had refused to be separated from my younger, nonverbal brother, because he couldn't speak for himself, I had been placed in substandard homes as a result. With the people who just took in disabled foster kids for the *extra* money. Yep. That was a thing. Karen has narcissistic personality disorder. She was hurting me and lying to the school and other adjacent adults because it made her feel good. She liked fooling people. It made her feel smart and powerful. Very few people saw her for what she was, and those who did couldn't overcome the tide against doing anything about it.

After third grade, the entire school system underwent a "redistricting" that sent me to another school. If you asked, I'm sure they'd tell you it had nothing to do with me. But everything else pointed to it specifically being my fault. Especially the parents of the kids who were part of Karen's phone tree and got moved from Best School too. Which "definitely wasn't about me, and was something they were always planning to do."

Bully continued his bullying campaign until I was too pretty to bully. Let's say I was sixteen. He did not like losing this outlet and tried to hold on as long as possible. He tried to get his friends to continue to hurt me too. One day, on the bus home, I was ignoring their taunts, so one of his friends ran up to me and slapped me in the face with a cake he'd had rotting in his backpack.

I had to walk home with old cake on my face and in my hair while the bus pulled away. What did the driver do? Nothing.

Years later, Bully's friend slid into my DMs trying to tell me how pretty I was now and asking whether I'd like to hook up during one of his trips to Atlanta where I was living at the time. He was engaged, but that didn't bother him if it didn't bother me. Of course. I had to pass. Yuck.

The kid who threw up when I told him about my childhood had a fun role to play here too. I told him the story of Bully and his main abuse partner, Bully 2. I shared that Bully 2 often gleefully told me everyone "could clearly see [I] was a Machado," and no matter what family I lived with, and whatever

I called myself, they'd make sure people always *knew*. Like I was trying to hide my Hispanicness. *Why did **that** bother them?!* Why, indeed. When I told Puke Kid the name of Bully 2, he became enraged and told me I needed to stop telling that story because he *knew* Bully 2. Bully 2 had been his camp counselor when he was a kid, and he was "a nice guy."

And "nice guys" defend other "nice guys." Even to their victims.

ADHD

The research around people like me—those with ADHD—is really not where it should be. There's no one I can talk to about my brain basically being feral on the inside and unwilling to heel when it comes to needing to perform normally for people.

One of the things the neurodiverse struggle with are lies. Whether something isn't literally true, not technically true, or just a flat-out falsehood, our brains will loudly scream our version of "Nope."

ADHD and autism are on the same neurodiversity spectrum. There's a ton of overlap. And quite honestly, I feel like I speak on this topic as an expert because I educate people on neurodiversity professionally. And personally. For over thirty years now.

What does ADHD mean to me? It means I forget my place a lot. I repeat myself. It was worse when I was a child because I had rambunctious untamable energy. I would know my life depended on me remembering to do something exactly the way Karen wanted it, and then I just couldn't remember.

I used to take everything literally. I thought everyone was speaking literally all the time. People even say "literally" when they mean "figuratively." But my brain was always processing things literally. My seven-year-old is the same way. He'll say:

"What time is it?"

"It's six," I'll answer, rounding up.

"No, it's 5:57!" he'll respond.

I've gotten feedback from terrible parents that he's being disrespectful but, no, he's being literal. That's what neurodiversity does. He's not assigning blame, or passing judgment; he's telling you factually:

"In case you didn't know, friend, it's actually 5:57."

Now I can see neurodiversity in others, and I can tell which kind of processing differences they might be experiencing just by talking to them. It's a weird gift I've developed. I see them standing in the gaps trapped by boundaries people say aren't there. I see the boundaries because I trip over them constantly. Usually, these boundaries are social rules that remain unspoken and turn into "everybody knows" statements. Or "people say" statements.

My whole life I was called "bossy," a "know-it-all." People complained that I talked too much and had no filter. Really, I had ADHD and was growing up around many adults who should not have been parents or teachers. If I had been a boy, they would've understood what was happening and gotten me support.

That messed with my feeling of safety a lot. Adults thought and told me I was bad because I didn't act the way they expected. But they didn't know anyone who had survived what I had survived. So, if I have a completely unique life experience intersecting with a different way of processing the world, how might that impact my ability to act in a way they find desirable? *They didn't know anyone like me. And they didn't even know that.* Because the human brain likes to be right.

ADHD-ers also have trouble with object permanence. It makes grief and processing grief an entirely different experience for me. I can ignore grief until it is brought back into my awareness again by some "trigger" experience. Then I have to live the entire memory from that point of view. When I explained it to a neurotypical[28] doctor once, he (of course) thought I was talking about "compartmentalization." That's not really the same thing, but

---

28 The opposite of neurodiverse is neurotypical. I just mean the folks who aren't on the spectrum. These folks are usually informing the "main" narrative of how humans process the world.

people knew nothing about ADHD when I was a kid. When I was a kid, doctors didn't even think little girls could have ADHD. They thought boys get ADHD and "have trouble sitting still" and girls have ADD and "chat a lot." Sounds like science?

People with neurodiversity have processing issues; we see everything. We can hear everything. The world isn't made for us. It's too loud, too bright, too hot, too cold, or too itchy, and that's painful. Let me give you an example: So you know how, if you're neurotypical, you can't feel your clothes on you? You can't hear the lights buzzing? You don't see the computer screen blinking? We can. Loudly. All at once. If I'm at a restaurant listening to you talk, I can also hear all the other conversations happening around us. Often situations that "cost" us the most, like crowds and fluorescent lighting, for example, cause our brains to become *overstimulated*. Our behavior and body language start to show the pain of that, but it somehow looks to neurotypical people like "defiance." And adults have strong opinions about defiant children to this day. Especially defiant foster children who get to go to nice schools.

And that definitely *did* have an impact on my overall ability to be successful, mostly because I was reminded every minute of every day that I wasn't living up to my "full potential." Which fit the narrative Karen was weaving for the phone tree perfectly.

I tried to explain what was going on with me thousands of times. It wasn't just that I couldn't pay attention; I literally could not learn a lesson not designed for me. I told them that I understood I was smart, but that I was struggling with ADHD.

"Well, someone thinks too highly of herself!" they'd say.

"But . . . you just said . . ." I'd try to say.

"Who do you think you are, you're a *foster kid*! You should be grateful you're here!" they'd retort.

Grateful for the opportunity to be gaslit, rejected, and abused. But they felt like they were bleaching me. Hiding the stains from others. They thought by just being there, my life trajectory would be changed in a positive way that they felt I didn't deserve. Maybe they were right. Gross and right.

So I grew up to fight for others like me. I don't get anything out of making space for people except that I feel like it's why I'm on earth. People always find me, and I always know exactly what to say that sets that person off onto a new course of interest or awareness. I think of it as adjusting their lens.

Why am I like this? Some of it is just me, individually. And some of it is ADHD. One of the fascinatingly common personality traits in ADHD-ers is this: We will jump into your situation with you to help you get out of it. If it's happening to you, it's happening to us. You have a hole in your boat? We're going to get in that boat with you and we're going to stay with you until we are both back to safety. I've been studying these commonalities all my life, knowing it couldn't just be me. I don't want to overstate things we all do, but I also don't want to take too much credit individually for things we all do.

ADHD-ers (and autistic people) are folks with brains that maximize pattern recognition. All human brains are good at pattern recognition, that's true, but for people on the ADHD/autism spectrum, it's taken to the extreme where our brains are able to accurately predict the outcomes of anything from the vibes at a party to, for me, human behavior.

Most folks who are neurotypical learn in levels. For example, they learn letters before they learn to read words. Then they learn to spell words. And then they learn to write sentences. One level informs the next and builds to a certain skill, such as knowing how to read and write. We call learning in levels "linear thinking." This is how most humans learn. Most humans keep information they have learned in their minds in sections, or silos.

Neurodiverse people like me keep the information they have learned in webs instead of silos. The information is all connected and informs our pattern recognition. In school situations, we have to teach ourselves. But that doesn't mean we learned *everything* on the lower levels first. *Because we can't see the levels.*

I was excellent in school at things I already understood the high-level concepts of; for example, history, social studies, and English. But I couldn't learn how to do math or chemistry in a classroom because I couldn't teach it to myself. Karen told me I was stupid and kept me from taking math classes whenever she could. Really, I think she was just jealous of me getting better at something that she once had been praised for in school. Math was *her* thing. And I couldn't learn it *alone*.

This created feelings of rejection in me. Everything did. I *was* being rejected. This is where rejection sensitive dysphoria (RSD) comes into play. According to the ADHD magazine *ADDitude*:

> RSD is extreme emotional sensitivity and pain triggered by the perception that a person has been rejected or criticized by important people in their life. It may also be triggered by a sense of falling short—failing to meet their own high standards or others' expectations.
>
> . . . **When this emotional response is internalized** (and it often is for people with RSD), it can imitate a full, major mood disorder complete with suicidal ideation. The sudden change from feeling perfectly fine to feeling intensely sad that results from RSD is often misdiagnosed as rapid cycling mood disorder.
>
> It can take a long time for physicians to recognize that these symptoms are caused by the sudden emotional changes associated with ADHD and rejection sensitivity, while all other aspects of relating to others seem typical. RSD is, in fact, a common ADHD symptom, particularly in adults.
>
> **When this emotional response is externalized**, it looks like an impressive, instantaneous rage at the person or situation responsible for causing the pain.[29]

The schools I went to didn't have people like me at them. They didn't know about foster kids. They used whatever TV narratives people were going by in the nineties to define me and my behavior through their own wrong lens. Limiting me and my future. Cutting my wings. Keeping me small. Regularly moving the goalposts around so their valuable time could go to teaching the

---

29   William Dodson, "How ADHD Ignites Rejection Sensitive Dysphoria," *ADDitude*, February 7, 2017, https://www.additudemag.com/rejection-sensitive-dysphoria-and-adhd/.

kids who were going places. Unlike me, I guess. I didn't think I could go to any of my teachers. I thought they were *in on my abuse*. Some of them were. Most of them weren't. But school was not a safe place. It's probably uncomfortable and awkward for everyone, but for neurodiverse kids, it can be excruciating.

Alcoholics Can't Stop

In my early teens, Karen decided the drama in her life was going to be that Willy was an alcoholic. He had always been an alcoholic, but I guess we were between family divorces and drama was low. Willy was the youngest son of four, and his Polish mother had been very ashamed to be pregnant with him late in life. He told the story a lot. It really stuck with him.

Willy's family owned a trucking company that did pretty well but came from "the wrong side of town." The entire town is fourteen square miles, but they grew up on opposite sides. Willy came from the Port side, where the river is. Karen was from the Highlands, and she *really* cared about it. Talk about never having been anywhere. So they grew up in this same town in the fifties. He was working class, and she was a prom queen. That was their whole story.

Willy ran his own commercial landscaping business and did pretty well. Not for as much as she needed to spend to fill the hole in Karen, but definitely enough. In fact, I remember one time we were on the way to the store when I was seven, and she asked him how much money he had.

"On me?" he asked. "I don't know, about a hundred bucks?"

"You have a hundred dollars?!" I asked. "Why didn't anyone tell me you were so rich!"

They had a great laugh at this at my expense and repeated it to people they meant to impress.

We're so well off that our foster kid thinks we're rich! LOL.

Maybe they just didn't know how poor *poverty* was. A lot of people don't. Seems weird that they missed the point of the story, huh?

But eventually his alcoholism stopped being something that made him easier to control and started becoming a problem for Karen.

And that's where this story begins.

"Di-anne-er!" Karen yelled up to me.

I was at the top of the spiral staircase that led to my Princess Prison. I slept in a tiny converted attic loft with no air-conditioning. There was a bed up there when DCFS was checking in, but they stopped checking in, so Karen gave the bed to someone else. The house was always full, and standards dropped when no one was looking. As one might expect.

I called my room my "Princess Prison" because Karen always told me it wasn't for *me* to enjoy but for the next little girl to enjoy once she was finally rid of me. Apparently, she also used its existence to gaslight everyone else who might one day hear of her abuse: that, in fact, I was treated like a princess. *Princess Prison.*[30] This is a very common abuse strategy and gives the victim the feeling that if she were to tell of her abuse, no one would care because it doesn't "look" the way people need abuse to look.

I poked my head out from the book I had "earned" time to read and looked down to her.

Books were my escape.[31]

"I'm just reading," I said. "You told me I could!"

"Di-anne-er! Get down here!"

Why did she say my name like that? Racism. I had tried to pronounce it for her about six thousand times; I told her it's "Dee-ah-nah" for Spanish, Italian, French, and Portuguese speakers or "Dye-anna" for English speakers. She repeatedly responded by letting me know this was America, *"where we don't push one for English."* Another favorite racist saying of hers.

Listen better, the other small-town adults around her advised. Of course.

---

30 Also her father died in that room at the base of the staircase.
31 Thanks to my TV-dad, LeVar Burton.

I skidded down the stairs, stood in front of her in the doorway, and shrugged expectantly.

What?

She considered me narrowly and indicated I should follow her to the front room silently. I did. When I got there, I found the three younger kids—Ted, Becky, and Chavonne—waiting and a disheveled and sniveling Willy looking ashamed and forlorn, sitting in the front doorway on the bench we used to put shoes on. It was maroon.

Great.

"Sit," Karen instructed.

I immediately sank into the couch, searching everyone's faces for some indication of what was happening, but no one would meet my eye. They were looking at the floor.

"Go ahead, Will," Karen prompted.

Will? She never called him Will. She called her son that. She's softening her speech to manipulate him, I realized. But why?

Find the danger! my ADHD brain warned.

He took a deep breath that seemed to suck the air out from *my* lungs and began:

"I wanted to apologize to you all. For the drinking," Willy said. "It's not fair and I'm going to change."

I looked over at Karen, who had tears streaming down her face.

I raised my hand.

Her look hardened immediately as she regarded my audacity, and I realized, too late, why a woman I thought was a soulless monster was somehow crying for someone she obviously hated. She wasn't. This was her martyr moment, and I was taking the attention from her.

I lowered my hand.

"Go ahead, sweetie," Willy said.

Too late.

"Will you be going to the meetings at the church?" I asked.

"What did you say?!" she sputtered.

"I just wondered if he would be doing the meetings for alcoholics at our church," I repeated quietly.

"No!" she shrieked. "Of course not!"

"No," Willy said more calmly. "We've decided we can take care of this as a family and we're going to take care of it privately."

"But—" I started.

"Kids!" Karen interrupted. "Go hug your father!"

Obediently, we all did.

When it was over, Karen followed me out of the conversation, like always, and then grabbed me by my shirt to stop me from escaping back to my Princess Prison.

I was always trying to escape her, and she was always finding new and more painful ways to stop me.

"We aren't like you. We don't need everyone to know everything about us," she sneered.

"Why do I need everyone to know everything about me?" I asked.

"That's a question you need to ask yourself!"

"No, I mean, I'm asking you. What makes you think that?"

This was always happening to me because of the ADHD. Or because of her narcissism. Or both.

"Well, you're always writing everything down in your little journals! I better not hear you breathe a word of this to your little friends!" she threatened.

"Why would I want my friends to know my dad is an alcoholic?"

"He's not!" she said. "Didn't you hear him?! He's quitting!"

As if that would make it so.

"He's an alcoholic. They can't just stop. It's an addiction," I said.

"Maybe not *your* drug-addicted parents!" she retorted. "Maybe you never gave them a good enough reason to quit!"

Her nuclear insult. And she pulled it out every time she felt inferior to me. Which really took the sting out of it.

"Look, I don't care what you think of my 'parents,'" I said, more calmly than I felt. "But I do know he can't quit by himself."

"Then why did you hug him?!" she snarled.

"You told me to," I reminded her.

A hug is forgiveness?

"Stupid, jealous b——h," she sneered. "You have no feeling left anymore because everyone took it away from you, didn't they? You crusty, heartless b——h."

She stormed off.

I was not quite a teenager that day, and Willy is still an alcoholic today. Even though his doctor told him in the early aughts that he would literally die if he didn't quit drinking. He still does. Because alcoholism is a disease, even if you don't want it to be. Even if it embarrasses you.

I tried to warn her. Not because I was trying to be a know-it-all but because I didn't yet understand there were some big feelings knotted up with some well-known facts at that point.

Because I already knew a lot about addiction, no?

Willy was actually pretty ambivalent toward me in the beginning. If not nice, at least human.

Once, when I was eight, Karen instructed me to clean up Chavonne and Becky's room. They had the nicest room in the house. All of their furniture matched, and they had gorgeous clothes from this boutique nearby called Peanut Butter and Jelly Kids. It's what it sounds like it might be. Matching furniture is important to foster kids because all of our bedrooms are temporary and thrown together. An afterthought. Wanted kids got planned bedrooms with matching furniture with their names stenciled on the wall. It was and would always be theirs.

I was sitting in front of their closet door, matching up all the tiny patent leather shoes. The bigger ones were Becky's and went on the right. The littler ones were Chavonne's and went on the left. Rows and rows of shoes. There I was, staring off into space, pretending the shoes were different people and giving them voices, when Karen came in to "check my progress." I had ADHD, so I always made very slow progress. When you give an ADHD-er a broad task like "clean your room," for them getting started can be paralyzing. She counted on it so she could go back to talking on the phone, shopping, or watching TV, and I'd be alone struggling to start or complete some random task or chore.

In her anger at seeing I had only finished the shoes, she beat me over and over with a coat hanger. A wire coat hanger. I was eight. I screamed and cried so horribly that Willy came into the room where she was beating me, took away the hanger, and threw it on the ground. Then he picked me up off the ground and plopped me onto the couch in the den, one room away, never uttering a word to her. Unfortunately, Willy just left me there alone and then left the house for Karen to come find me. Like he knew she would. Like the coward he was.

Everyone reading this would have done more and I would've too.

Karen waited until she heard him leave to come get me back. Like the coward *she* was.

We both listened for his diesel engine to turn over and heat up. Sure enough, a few minutes later, the engine got quieter, and Willy was off in a huff to go drink at a local watering hole.

Enter Karen.

We both knew what was going to happen next. My beating would continue.

Sure enough, she grabbed me by my ponytail, dragged me by it back into the room where I hadn't made enough progress, and then beat me bloody.

I have no idea whether they ever got into it about him saving me from her, but he never did it again. He never interfered, never intervened, and never stuck up for me. However, she did seem to get a little more cautious and beat me less when he could hear. Yes, only less.

I have no idea why nobody ever stopped her. In fact, the opposite. You may be surprised to learn this if this isn't your path, but if you came from an abusive family, you know. It's often one person who gets to be the brunt of this type of abuse and everyone else accepts it on your behalf, happy the blight hasn't fallen on them. Some of them will go so far as to *help* the abuser abuse. Some lesser offenders need to believe wholeheartedly in your guilt in order to justify their action. Or inaction as the case might be. It's usually *everyone* who treats one person as worthy of disdain and abuse. They *have to*.

Safe Spaces

About halfway through my freshman year of high school, I discovered we had an on-site counselor. Not a guidance counselor. A therapist, apparently. Or at least, that's what I heard. She had short black hair, bright red lipstick, and often wore white tights with apples printed on them.

"How do you get to go to her?" I asked a teacher once.

"You get special permission from the nurse or the office."

"How do you get that?" I asked.

"You go to the nurse or the office and tell them why you think you need to see the counselor. She works with kids who are having problems, like if their parents are divorcing or something."

"Oh," I said. *Like if their parents are divorcing.*

I considered the matter dropped.

I had to walk past her office daily, which was adjacent to an open seating area, so a lot of sad-looking girls would hang out there waiting to cry to the counselor after their boyfriends broke up with them.

That happened a lot.

But this therapy wasn't for me. Nothing seemed to be.

I heard every reason. People whose jobs were to spot and catch abuse told me all my abuse was in the past. I was regularly reminded at assemblies about inappropriate touching by adults on children that I wasn't who they were talking about when they were discussing victims. And they told me they already knew about my abuse and didn't want to open a new complaint from every outreach assembly.

In the second grade.

But the abuse was never over, and there were always several new instances throughout my life. And once I learned that a behavior was abusive, sexually abusive, or otherwise coercive, I tried to tell. I tried to get help. I tried to find someone who could help make it stop.

But they didn't help me. They just got *me* to stop reporting it to them. Because they'd been clear: their help (and funded resources) were Not. For. Me.

I Forgot

When I was fourteen, Karen once angrily asked me to grab her something off the attic stairs, where she kept an unsafe volume of items stacked. I don't remember exactly what she asked for, although that was also the problem that day, ironically.

When I climbed the stairs to the attic, my ADHD interfered and ate the thought. *POP!* I completely forgot what she had asked me to get.

As I stood there looking spaced and trying to remember, that voice bellowed from behind me.

"WHAT ARE YOU DOING?!"

She'd snuck up behind me to startle me, which was a favorite thing of hers for some reason. Right after she yelled, she realized I hadn't yet retrieved whatever she had wanted, flew into a rage, and hit me with a broom she had hung on the wall going up to the attic.

She hit me as hard as she could with it. Over and over.

"Stop! Please!" I cried. "I'm sorry! I just forgot! I forgot . . ."

She got even angrier, noticing that the angle of the steps was limiting her ability to swing the broom to do the kind of damage she was looking to do to me, and changing strategies trying to spear me with it instead.

"STUPID . . . F——G . . . GIRL! WORTHLESS . . . F——G . . . RET——D!"[32]

The only thing that stopped her was the sound of the storm door swinging open downstairs. Someone had entered the busy house.

"Clean yourself and this mess you made up," she said, as she put down the broom. Then she slammed the attic door shut.

I cried silently for a few minutes. Then I cleaned up the mess she'd made.

Once I was finished, I snuck out the attic door and crept to a safe place, careful not to show my tearstained face to anyone. She wouldn't like someone asking me what was wrong or what had happened.

Not that anyone would have asked.

Not in *that* house.

The next day, I showed up to school covered in bruises and ran into an older friend of mine, the seventeen-year-old captain of the school's color guard team. The first thing she did was ask me what had happened. I tried to brush her off and say they were sports injuries as I'd been instructed by Karen many times before. But she knew it wasn't true and pressed me to tell her the truth. Not seeing any harm in doing so, I told her.

She took it badly. So badly, apparently, that she wept uncontrollably about it in class. And while nobody seemed to mind when I cried or tried to report abuse, that was not the case when she did. Her teacher asked her what had happened. She reported the whole story to him. And he reported the whole thing. They both did the right thing.

Which is nice, I guess.

About halfway through the day, I got name-checked over the intercom.

"Diana Machado to the counselor's office, please. Diana Machado, go to the counselor's office please."

It took me exactly thirty seconds to get really nervous. I had never been to her before, so this was some kind of escalation. I could only think of one thing I had done differently that day.

"Crap," I mumbled, in realization.

---

32 Apologies for the ableist term; it's a quote.

I'd told.

When I arrived at the counselor's office, I found Karen sitting opposite an empty seat. She regarded me coolly, her back to the counselor.

"Sit here, sweetie."

All the air was sucked out of the room.

When I sat, she put her hand on my right thigh and squeezed. Hard. Then she left it there.

I almost didn't hear what the counselor was saying, my brain still piecing together what had happened and trying to come up with a better lie. *Run!*

". . . and of course your friend comes from a nice family, so she was very upset, you shouldn't blame *her*[33] . . . so I brought your mom in here so we could talk it out . . ." the counselor said.

What?

I could feel all the blood drain from my face and build in my thighs, preparing me to run. But there was nowhere to go, so I just nodded along, trying to minimize the damage and survive.

Karen saw me start to open my mouth and hurried to talk over me.

"Well, I don't know if you know, Mrs. Therapist, but Diana is in foster care with us . . ."

Mrs. Therapist looked stunned but intrigued. Too intrigued. She leaned forward, looking me over.

"I'm surprised we haven't met before—"

"Yes, well, she has to see *so many* professionals. We didn't want to put additional pressure on her. She just wants to be normal, and I'm sure DCFS wouldn't want her progress set back."

I was seeing no one at this point. Not a single professional. Karen was the secretary treasurer for the local foster care leadership group, had gained some leverage over local DCFS, and had everyone fooled into thinking I didn't need to see any professionals.

---

33 I don't blame this friend and I still love her. She trusted the system to work the way nice people think it does.

I hadn't seen a social worker since I was eleven. Karen convinced one not to come back, and apparently, they were a little overwhelmed down there, so they didn't bother sending anyone else. I also hadn't seen my appointed therapist since I was eleven. Karen convinced a social worker that therapy made me feel different from the other kids and that I was "all better now." And with tight budgets on top of busy schedules, they didn't fight her.

I was fully isolated.

"Yes, well," the counselor continued, "we need to discuss what Diana has reported to her friend."

"Diana," Karen prompted. "Why don't you step outside, so I can talk with Mrs. Therapist."

I could run.

But there was nowhere to go. And no one knew that better than I did.

I took one last sad look at the counselor, with her apple tights and her eager, golden retriever expression, and thought:

No match for Karen. This is how she likes them.

I stepped into the hallway and listened for a few minutes.

"Sorry, I hate to talk in front of her, but you know she was sexually assaulted by her mother's boyfriend, right? Maybe *all* of them."

The counselor gasped.

Great.

"Oh yes!" Karen continued. "It's *so* tragic, and now the poor thing can't tell the difference between what is happening now and what's happened before!"

Apple Tights clucked. Too interested. No help.

And I just floated away.

As I waited outside the counselor's office, the bell rang and classes changed. I tried to look normal as the other kids walked by as if I had a "normal" reason to be there. Maybe I had a bad boyfriend. But then Karen came out, thundering my trauma to the echoing hallway.

She loved to tell new people. It was her absolute favorite thing. She loved the attention. Nothing made her feel more like a saint, and got her treated like one, like telling people how bad it had been for me where I'd come from.

The counselor looked pitiful. Clearly, she'd been crying. Then she told me it had been nice to meet me. I nodded.

As we walked away, Karen put her arm around me and leaned in close:

"Did you see how easy that was? She didn't even believe you. She was disgusted by you. You'll be lucky if she doesn't tell every single teacher in this school that you're a crazy sl—t-liar.[34] She thinks you should take tomorrow off and come back to school on Monday. After a *family break*."

Three and a half days for her to show me just how angry I'd made her.

Sometimes I think back to that counselor and wonder whether she has since put anyone else in mortal danger because she didn't know a lick about foster care, domestic violence, child abuse, or narcissism. But she definitely endangered *my* life, and I do blame her as a trained professional. And if she wasn't trained, she shouldn't have been in that position. She was in her fifties. I'm in my thirties and I know better.

As you can imagine, I never went anywhere near Mrs. Therapist again. I walked the entire long way around the school just to avoid her. And she never once sought me out.

She did, however, tell every single teacher in explicit detail what had happened to me, just as Karen promised she would.

I know because I was close with the writing teacher who got the update.

And that's why I never told again at school.

Because there's a limit to safe spaces. And it's right at the place where someone *else* gets to decide whether you're worthy of feeling safe.

---

34 "Sl—t" was in just about every insult string. Like a child who has just learned how to swear but doesn't have a lot of vocabulary yet.

Pretty Now

At sixteen, I was a gawky kid at school and nobody paid much attention to me. Over the summer, however, my body developed quickly and I returned to school in a woman's body the following school year.

A lot of us have had the experience, I assume. It comes with an influx of sudden and unwanted attention. This is a particularly difficult period in the life of someone like me, however, because unwanted sexual attention from grown men can be incredibly destabilizing. It's just gross and not at all a compliment. But that's what started happening. A lot. It made me consistently feel unsafe in my own skin. In school spaces. Even Karen noticed it.

As a mother today, I would defend my children against unwanted sexual attention from adult men, but having read this far, I suspect you know Karen didn't see it that way.

Karen saw the attention I was getting as power. Not *her* power but something that *limited* her power over me. It made her jealous that I began getting attention. It enraged her. It incensed her. The attention I didn't want. That I wished would stop. And she was jealous of it.

How does a narcissist react when they are jealous of you? They try to tear you down. They make everything about them. They lie about you. They try to turn everyone against you. They engage in *negging*. (If you're unfamiliar with the term, negging happens when someone tries to get your attention by insulting you until you defend yourself to them.)

In my case, Karen kept making up narratives that I must be "acting like a sl—t" to be receiving all the attention I didn't ask for and had no control over.

But I didn't subscribe to her version of morality because, if it exalted her and hurt me, I wasn't really interested in hearing the word "infallible" to describe *that*.

And if I was going to be treated as if *her* reality was *my* reality, I needed to figure out what this unused power was. And own it.

Once we were walking through a local shopping mall getting a gift for a family event. I was just walking and she became outraged out of nowhere. Her reason? I was walking like I wanted attention. What does that even mean?!

"Diana!" she hissed, always loud enough for anyone nearby to hear her shaming me. "I am sick of you walking like you want *this* attention! You walk around like everyone is looking at you! It's despicable!"

A few people actually were looking because public shaming was (and is . . .) totally a thing that attracts attention in suburbia, apparently.

I looked around, inwardly burning with shame but outwardly deciding to take the "dumb teenager" approach.

"But they *are* all looking . . . ?"

People actually snickered. *Good*, I thought.

"THAT'S NOT THE POINT!"

"Well, if they're going to look whether I want them to or not, I'm going to act like I deserve it. It's not *my* fault *they* look," I said, motioning toward the gawkers.

"*It is your* fault because you're a SL—T!"[35] she said.

This was when I noticed the gawkers had thinned out, starting to feel sorry for me and shame for watching this all unfold. (And possibly feeling a little shame for *not doing anything* to help.)

She noticed it too.

---

35 See what I mean? No imagination.

"Let's go! We're going to be late! I'm sick of your sh—t! I'm going to tell everyone you're the reason we're late!" she complained, suddenly on the move again.

I made eye contact with a few straggling observers, and we all kind of smiled sadly. One nodded at me.

You got this.

A Changing Tide

It used to be that when she shamed me in public—weirdly always for a crowd in a store—the spectators all agreed with her. That would give her the opportunity to spin it as "*I don't know who you think you are, acting this way. We aren't giving in to raising bad kids, even if you don't like it, foster kid!*"

People would nod their approval at her when she'd say whatever version of that sentiment she'd deliver for the crowd.

Right on, lady! I hate these "everybody gets a trophy" kids!

I've often heard it said by folks who have had abuse in their histories that their parents would wait for the car to unleash physical abuse. Not narcissist parents. They do a show for the store, then beat you in the car, and *then* beat you more severely when you get home. Actually, I guess everyone does a show for the store.

There's apparently something universal about the stress of the store that puts people into these mindsets where they need to lash out explosively.

I retell this story because it illustrates my growing awareness of unseen and very unspoken social norms. I had developed into "a pretty girl" quickly. And that changed our power dynamic. In her mind, I was young and pretty in a gender where young and pretty is the only known power position. In my mind, *knowledge* was power, people are power, and I wasn't *super* impressed with being thought of as sexually desirable by adult men.[36] Call it trauma from past sexual abuse.

---

36 By the way, "catcalling" (ick) ends for most women when they are no longer teenage girls. Feel free to check my math with the women in your life if you want to see someone have a really sad realization.

But with me suddenly becoming pretty, Karen also started realizing she could gain social cookies living vicariously through me and continuing to control as much of my life as she could. Of course, there wasn't really much choice about whether I would cooperate with her plans and dramas. I would. I was her pawn.

What I got in exchange for being her pawn in the beginning was less physical abuse. After all, if I were bruised, I would be less pretty and she couldn't use me or show me off. She wanted people to see me. Because she *needed* people to see her.

But that dynamic got old fast.

I soon realized everything she was doing was for her benefit, alone, and left me having to defend her choices and behavior from the enabling accomplice position. She didn't harbor less anger. She wasn't less narcissistic. She just couldn't take all of it out on me because I'd be the bruised girl and not the pretty girl who got her the attention she so desperately desired.

So she'd take it out on others more, and her abuse became more impactful for people who had already outgrown it, like my foster sister, Marie.

Marie has a daughter one month older than me, Jessica. Karen loved to pit Jessica and me against each other to punish Marie.

Move the Car

When I came on the scene at age seven, Marie and Karen were already fighting. Marie and Jessica had been living at Karen's home since before Marie was married to her first husband. When they got married, everyone moved into a new house together. Marie wanted everyone to live together as one big happy family.

You might remember that Karen had miscarried a pregnancy that was due around the time I was born. She never let me forget that, reminding me every chance she got that I would never matter to them or anyone as much as a daughter born to them because I was less and came from less. All I could do was aspire to earn what a real daughter would have received by "working harder to earn my place." Then again, her "real" daughter, Marie, was treated the same as me, so *maybe* this whole line of thinking was just another way for Karen to abuse and control me. Maybe . . .

Karen and Marie would have been pregnant at the same time; Karen with the daughter she lost and Marie with Jessica. Karen abused Marie the way she abused me, so Jessica became something Karen and Marie fought about frequently. I was placed in the home after *that* battle was lost by Karen.

Jessica and I were raised mostly together, outwardly. Inwardly, our experiences were worlds apart in our two different homes. But we were together for "the family" milestones, of course with the exception of when Marie and Karen were mad at each other for whatever reason. Like I said, Karen and Marie fall out every ten years or so, and one of those times occurred when Jessica and I were teenagers.

I can't remember what triggered that falling out initially, but I do remember that it ended with Karen spending about $1,000 buying me clothes so she could take pictures to brag to Marie about how well she treated me. We had an entire dress-up montage, and she took photos to show everyone. (Then she returned all the clothes but one skintight maroon dress I hated, naturally.)

It was really important to Karen for me to tell everyone all about our shopping and picture spree in a certain way. She had me rehearse it over and over again. That was a big thing with her: rehearsing *The Story* we tell people about whatever lie she had me telling people from time to time. This time I had to rehearse it as she drove me to color guard practice. If I got one word wrong, she'd interrupt and correct me. Over and over. All the way to practice, and she even had me sit in the car—at that point after practice had already started—until I got it *just right* before I could get out of the car.

When I finally got out of the car at drop-off and tried to shut the minivan sliding door to drown out her continued correcting, she angrily jerked the car forward and parked it on my foot. And it wasn't like she hadn't intended to do that. What else could she have *intended* to do when she sped forward and stopped short?

"MOVE THE CAR!" I screamed.

She smirked. "I guess you aren't storming off today, huh?"

"The car is parked on me!"

"Tell me the story how I want you to tell it and I will let you go," she replied calmly.

I retold the *thousands of dollars in clothes* story so it would get back to Marie. She moved the car. And sped off.

As she sped away, I sat on the nearby sidewalk thinking about how desperate Karen was for her own daughter to think she was capable of loving someone else—just not Marie because Marie was *unlovable*. Karen wanted Marie to know she was capable of being a parent who got involved and cared about *a* daughter—just someone. Again, not Marie. *Marie was the problem* in their relationship. But I had become the shining example of her love and selfless parenting. And as I was sitting outside—a human child with broken toes and permanent damage to my foot—the irony wasn't lost on me. And that is the narcissist's version of love.

Unfortunately, once I realized I was starting to become complicit in her dramas just to stay out of her path of abuse, I couldn't unknow that.

I think that type of realization is a real turning point for most people in my particular hell.

It certainly was for me.

Do I oppose her? How will she punish me? Do I have a choice?

Ultimately, I knew I couldn't let her use me that way and somehow not be at least partially responsible for the damage she did to others.

Because that's how abusers stay abusing—with the help of their enablers.

Not Worthy of an Apology

On a color guard trip to Hawaii (that *I* paid for), I got a pretty serious sunburn. Volunteers joined the trip to take care of the kids. Sometimes I'd pretend those moms were my mom too. Sports moms; everyone does that. That's supposedly what they're there for. So you can perform at the highest level of competition as a child.

If they see you as a child.

I found one of the moms who knew me, and I threw my arms around her, smiling.

"Mama, I have a sunburn!" I joked.

This woman looked me in my face and asked, "Why don't you go tell somebody who cares?" and then walked off.

Later she apparently thought better of it, and possibly assumed I'd tell Karen, so she apologized *to Karen* for her overstep. Blaming me, she explained she had been hot and stressed and that I'd been hanging all over her; always so needy.

But I hadn't told Karen what she'd said. I'd already *blamed myself* for that rejection. I'd already blamed myself for reaching out to a mother. I'd already blamed myself.

Those are words I would never say as a mother now to someone else's kid—or my own.

Karen was enraged I hadn't told her. She had no opportunity to use it to her advantage, manipulate this person, or tell anyone else and make this person feel bad. I just absorbed it on her behalf. Like I always did.

But that's what I mean about Karen's adult enablers; they hurt me right along with her and never felt a moment's shame.

Sports Mom didn't even apologize to me. She apologized to the person she felt was worthy of an apology.

Which was not me.

High School

High school was a nightmare for me. Maybe high school is a nightmare for most everyone, but this time in my life was overwhelmingly oppressive and awful. I was bullied nonstop for my clothes, my "weird, wild" hair, which Karen never brought me to have cut or kept (of course), the fact that I never got to eat lunch, and so many other things that were out of my control.

The kids who had known me the longest called me "Dirty Diana," a nickname they gave me after discovering I was in foster care when I first came to school with them in their ultra-white suburb.

Just like before, Karen still felt like I "shouldn't need to do homework after school." It was really starting to cut into my chores time, and she felt that, if they couldn't teach me what they needed to teach me in the allotted time, I needed to take easier classes.

I know now she felt inferior to me and knew I was already smarter than she was, so she made it her mission to hold me back in as many ways as she could. She had me get a job, and sometimes two, to make sure I was using my off-from-school hours in a way that suited her. If I wasn't doing chores at home, or playing sports she forced me to play (in my case, color guard, softball, band etc.), I was working (and she was keeping the money).

Making me take easier classes and forcing me to play sports was all about her. She wanted to be a part of a community of sports moms and the prestige that offered her. When I couldn't do both, she called my guidance counselor and had me put in special education classes in math and sciences so I could keep my grades up. I couldn't play sports without having the qualifying grades, per school policy. So easier classes it was.

I also had to take typing instead of computer science because she believed women should only have access to the types of education that made them marriage material. Or maybe she just believed that about me. I was taken out of algebra and put into "life skills math." Taught to write checks and figure out how much money one should spend a month on rent. (Supposedly, it's a quarter of your monthly income. So totally wrong and ultimately useless in every single objective way.)

All the kids in those classes that weren't developmentally delayed were juvenile delinquents, so fights broke out often. Once, a teacher threw a desk at a student when the student rushed his desk to attack him. When I told the guidance counselor about it and asked to change back to algebra, she told me not to be so dramatic and then said my skin was like porcelain and remarked how lucky I was.

"Most Machados are dark!" she'd called after me when I disgustedly tried to exit. "That's not racist, it's just true!"

*Well, if **you** say so.*

The only times I got complimented by most adults it was backhanded, with some demand for a behavior modification, specifically referencing my history in foster care, my racial ambiguity, or straight up misogyny. Just like my foster mother had taught them.

Apparently, abusing foster kids makes a lot of people who aren't where they want to be feel better.

When I asked about the SATs and my college options, I found out Karen had already called and convinced the guidance counselor that I absolutely was incapable of anything beyond junior college. I wasn't even allowed to sit the tests.

"Look at your grades," Guidance said. "Your only option is community college. Then, if you want, you can go to a four-year school from there."

These were lies and she knew it. Just as I did when she said it to me. Because science. It was the early 2000s, not the 1950s. We already knew *most* kids drop out of junior college and don't graduate from a four-year program. For foster kids? Even fewer. Statistically irrelevant.

My grades in classes for my level were excellent other than in math and science. But I was smarter than some of my teachers. People don't like when you know that. I'm not sure why. It's measurable. I know plenty of people who are smarter than I am. *Much* smarter than I am. It's not that big a deal. I have many flaws. I can't squish a spider. Or swim in a large pool without thinking there might be a shark in there. I could go on and on.

When I was a junior, I had trouble with chemistry, and I was asked to stay after school one day to get extra help from the science teacher. When I met him after school, in conversation, he asked me how old I was.

"I'm seventeen," I told him.

"Oh," he said. "Have you ever been in a porno?"

"A what?" I asked.

"A porno," he repeated.

Like he was ordering a sandwich.

"I was watching a porno last night while my wife was at book club, and this chick getting f———d looked just like you."

"Oh," I said, embarrassed. "No, I've never had a boyfriend, and I haven't done porn."

To this day, I have no idea why I said that.

"I really want to show it to you," he said. "I'm sure it's you."

"But it's not me," I said again.

"Sure it is," he said, inching to sit closer to me.

I looked at him quizzically, just no idea what to say next. If I kept pushing that it wasn't me, would he fail me? Why was this happening?

"Tell you what," he said, eyes looking to the open doorway. "Meet me tomorrow before school. I'll be in the weight room. No one else will be there, and I'll bring a school TV and the movie and you can prove to me it isn't you."

"I'm not sure I can get here that early," I said. "I work late and I'll have to catch a ride from someone."

"Well, you can be here, or you can get an F," he said.

"Why are you watching porn?" I asked. "I thought your wife was pregnant."

Again, I'm seventeen. I don't know. I figured they were having sex if she was pregnant. All my practical knowledge of sex came from health class at this point. Or abuse. Which is what *this was.*

"She is. She trapped me with another baby and now I never get any," he answered.

"Any what?" I asked.

"Any *sex, obviously,*" he said.

I nodded and tried to look like I understood while having absolutely no idea why I was hearing all this. Feeling scared and on unequal footing.

"So I'll tear up this grade and I'll see you tomorrow morning?" he asked.

"Sure," I said, grabbing my stuff and bolting for the door.

I had a sinking feeling where this was going from the "no one will be there" comment. I was awake all night. I was so scared that I didn't fall asleep until early morning and then slept through my alarm. His class was right by the door to come into the school, so when I got there I tried to look as hurried and late as possible. He looked up from his desk when he saw the door open, and I mouthed "sorry" in his direction. He nodded and went back to teaching the other children.

I know now why he picked me, as an adult who has been through half a lifetime of therapy. I was being targeted for abuse because I was a "throwaway kid," and predators can always spot a throwaway kid who doesn't have someone looking out for them.

Later that week he cornered me again:

"Hey, so let's reschedule," he said, "so we can watch *your* movie together. Because I'm feeling *really hurt* that I had to look like an idiot pushing that huge TV back from the weight room after not getting laid."

Great.

"Sure," I said. "I have practice every open hour this week when I'm not working after school, so we'll have to work it out later."

These were lies, but whatever. I just wanted to get out of there.

"Great," he said, "I'm looking forward to it."

I *immediately* started only-at-school-dating one of my largest and loudest friends who was also in that class to get him off me. Today I wish I had told this guy that, but I didn't know whether he'd be cool. So, Guy, I'm sorry I was a terrible high school girlfriend who wouldn't have sex with you. I was using you as a shield because I believed the patriarchy that men were a threat to me, and the only thing I could do about it was get a bigger man to protect me from them.

Now I'm old enough to know if I had a problem in my neighborhood with bobcats attacking, I wouldn't adopt a grizzly to deal with the problem, ami-right? I'd still get eaten. And do I care which one kills me? Not really. Still dead.

Startlingly, this type of predatory and grooming behavior by teachers wasn't *that* uncommon at my high school. One of the math teachers was openly dating one of the juniors who got held back due to her learning disabilities. They couldn't do anything about it because she was eighteen, but he wasn't invited back for her senior year. And *everyone knew* that.

They still do.

One of the *other* science teachers bragged often about how he married his student right after her graduation day. They'd been having sex while she was a student. When she couldn't legally have consented. He hated me, and the feeling was definitely mutual. I knew he was an old, entitled scumbag and I acted accordingly. Because I have an uncanny sense when it comes to pedophiles. And they do not like being seen by me. But you know me, I have to fight every battle. *I'm in progress.* More on him later.

There was one bright spot in high school: a teacher named Dan Camilli.

I want to talk about Dan Camilli specifically because he went out of his way to protect me from what was going on around me to the extent that he knew about it. He taught eastern religions, global perspectives, and a few types of history. I took every class he offered. He was a detailed storyteller, and he had lived an amazing life of travel and experiences already at the point when I knew him. He told me about how, when he was in school, he used to cut boring classes to go to the library at Harvard and just read. I took on that policy of cutting classes to go to the nearest off-campus library to read. It's a good policy to use in moderation if you have ADHD and can't sit through a class that day. He gave me books to devour, music to listen to, and poetry he thought I might identify with. I've read thousands of books because he demanded it of me. He saw and heard me as a safe adult.

One day in my senior year, he pulled me aside and said:

"This is not forever. All of this will be but a brief moment in time in a grand life you will lead. You are much bigger than this place. Leave this behind as soon as you graduate. But DO graduate."

I took that to heart and promised I would. Eventually, of course, I did all those things.

A teacher like Mr. Camilli can do more than just educate a kid going through what I went through, just as what the science teacher was doing could have damaged me forever.

Ultimately, all the books I'd read started a fire in me and echoed each other in one inescapable truth: the life I was living was not okay, it was not normal, and it wasn't my fault it was like this.

Mr. Camilli and I are still in touch. I joked he could pick his own fake name for this book, and he picked some dad-joke name like Mr. Incognito. But people who did right by me should get their flowers. And Dan Camilli was a good teacher.

He didn't just show me how to learn; he shifted the way I thought about how to live.

So, thanks, Mr. Incognito. Did you hear I met Jane Goodall? I know! She was tiny but enormous just like His Holiness the Dalai Lama. He wears a visor on stage, and it does nothing to detract from the awe of how you experience His presence. They were both my height! It made me feel like people my size could reach amazing feats of humanity.

And I kept my promise, like I keep *all* my promises.

But seriously; thanks, Dan.

For the Love of Women

"**Y**ou just want to argue!" Karen accused.

"I don't want to argue," I said calmly, gray rocking[37] her.

"Yes! You do! Well, *I* don't care! Everyone already knows you're not *my* daughter! They won't give you what you want!" she sneered.

Her favorite way to hurt me. I wasn't *her* daughter. Not now at sixteen, and not all the days before this one when I had worked tirelessly to "earn" her love. I had tried. I truly had.

"I don't want to argue," I repeated.

"Well, *I'm* not stupid," she said.

Whoops.

Not smart enough to stop using *that* setup. I love her narcissism. It's the perfect way to hurt her back. She wants to be respected and feared and thought of as cunning. And to her children, who she purposefully kept weak through lies and constant manipulation, she is. But not to me. Dunking on Karen became my literal favorite teenage pastime.

"Obviously you are because you aren't understanding me. I don't want to argue because it's not an argument. I am who I am, I was born this way, and

---

37 Gray rocking is a type of behavior you employ to keep a narcissist from hurting you if you can't go no-contact. It's a kind of behavior modification that doesn't add gas to their fire. Basically, you are acting like a boring, gray rock.

I honestly don't care what a bunch of landscapers and ex-cheerleaders sleeping with each other's partners in secret so they can maintain the moral high ground on Sunday have to say about it."

Her mouth was agape. She sputtered.

Too slow, I thought. So I twisted the knife. I was done having this conversation, and she was going to remember it.

"Why? Are you planning to move *your* husband back into *your* bedroom? 'Sanctity of marriage' and all? What? I can't hear you?"

"B——h," she spat.

"Classy," I retorted.

I'm not sorry, but I'm a work in progress.

I'm bisexual. I always have been. I've always known it. I've always been *out*. Everyone who knew me in high school knew I had an "I kiss girls" T-shirt I had made. Just to be out.

"Contrarian," Karen had called me.

"Mary Quite Contrary," Marie had said, laughing.

Whatever.

But they didn't see what I saw—kids at school who were being degraded every single day by having to be less of themselves, less human, and just less. The ones who couldn't hide who they were like I could. Like I *easily* could. Well, forget them. I don't hide. I was prepared to defend who I was. I was already doing that every day anyway. I was sick of the way they treated my friends. At least the abuse would be *for* something.

Around that same time, I started feeling like the best way to let people know I had other interests was to put a poster of two women kissing on my Princess Prison wall. It's the one you're thinking of and I have no regrets, Queer People. Karen hated it and told me so regularly.

"You just want attention," she accused.

"Why would *this* bring me attention?" I asked.

"You *know*[38] why!" she said.

---

38 If you're neurodiverse, the thing she is specifically trying to get me to do is acknowledge the patriarchy and what she thought was my place upholding it. But, nah.

"No, I think you should tell me," I said, baiting her.

At school, I was also friends with every LGBTQ+ person on campus, so I started bringing folks around. A lot of them had also been raised in "less traditional" settings and weren't really there to judge my mess. They made me feel normal. Many of them had more practiced ways of dealing with narcissists than I had at that point. They taught me gray rocking.

"Do you *have* to bring *them* around?" Karen complained.

"Who?" I asked.

"*Those types of people*. Do you just *attract* them?"

"Do I just attract good-looking, open-minded, well-read people who care about me, you mean?"

"You know what I mean."

"Yes. I think we both know what you mean."

By that time, as way too many people put it, my "boobs went from nonexistent to porn star." And it all happened over one summer. Yes, if you're wondering aloud why I phrase it like that, I'm **repeating it** for posterity. That's what people told me. When I was a human child. Goaded on by my foster mother. I knew *no women* who knew their worth. None. Every adult woman I knew was suffering under the dual consciousness of patriarchy; knowing in her mind that she is a full person, and yet having to operate in the world as less human. That's a wide chasm to close day to day. Minute to minute. And keep other girls in line should they think that they too deserve to be their whole selves. That's a pretty big mind trick. People joked at me that I was like Dolly Parton.

"I wish!" I always used to say. People looked really confused at that. People don't get me.

Because how long have we *known* about Dolly, y'all? A long time.

Anyway. Like Dolly (dare I?!), I had big boobs, and I was going to use them. You're already looking without my permission; I might as well get something out of this forced arrangement. Thus, my "I kiss girls" T-shirt was born. My friends were being abused in the hallways, in the locker rooms, and everywhere teachers pretended they couldn't see. When teachers weren't actively participating themselves.

So I just walked my gay friends to class and took the tardy.

Pull up, I guess. What else could they do to me?

Today, my friend Jarrett remembers this as the moment he realized he could be himself, and he says that I was the first person who made him feel safe as himself. I don't love that narrative because I didn't do anything any *decent* person should have done.

I often say I wasn't really raised into a culture by people; I was more or less raised into humanness through books, movies, and music. Because of that, I wasn't ever really "in the closet." With my grandmother's love of Bea Arthur, we watched *The Golden Girls* together and laughed and discussed the social situations the girls were dealing with at the time. I knew what she thought of me.

A lot of my queer women[39] friends remark that they didn't know any gay girls in high school. This is because of what social psychologists call "compulsory heterosexuality." All female-presenting people are socialized to seek relationships with men. Boys are taught what it is to be men and how to use women for their own needs. *Boys will be boys.* At a ridiculously young age, girls are sexualized by grown men.

I've always been bisexual. When I say that, sometimes I get static; it goes like this:

"Well, Di, don't you mean pansexual[40]?" someone will ask.

"No, I mean bisexual," I'll answer.

"Well, Di, I never took you for a transphobe!" they'll retort.

Great.

"The prefix 'bi' means two! That means you're only attracted to binary people!" they'll declare, having proudly vanquished me with words.

No. And the wrongness of that contributes to what we call *bi-erasure*.

The prefix "bi" in bisexual refers to (1) attraction to genders that are the same as self, and (2) attraction to genders that are not the same as self. I know that because I'm bisexual. Imagine having the audacity to think they

---

39 And femmes: I always mean to include everyone. Trans+ women are women.

40 I have no beef with actual pansexuals; I have beef with definitions of pansexuality that misrepresent bisexuality. Carry on, consenting adults!

should argue with me about it, right? The actual motto of the bisexual community is "regardless of gender" and has been since about the 1970s (or sooner, some date it to the 1950s). Straight people finding out about trans+ people was not what brought them into existence. It's just what lets them exist within the collective consciousness and have a place within society. *And that's a much longer book.*

Bisexuality also does not mean I am 50 percent attracted to men and 50 percent attracted to women as some obviously wrong assumptions suggest. That's another transphobic thing that comes from the majority narrative. It's not *our* experience. Unfortunately, I see some LGBTQ+ folks not always understanding the difference out there in the world, so I'll be super direct in this section.

Bi and pan can and are used interchangeably within the community.

Imagining that I'm transphobic because I say I'm bisexual means you recently found out about trans+ or nonbinary people. Whether I am attracted to someone of the same gender as me or a different gender than me, that already includes trans+ or nonbinary people. They're already included. This assumption is asking me to be responsible for closing the gap between the real vocabulary of a community and an outsider's awareness of it. We aren't a sound bite for once-a-year allyship; we live here. And trans+ people have been part of the Queer Community for all the time I've been here and certainly before me. As for me? I've dated *all kinds* of grown folks.

Actually, while I'm here, I want to talk about gatekeeping in the lesbian community because bisexual and pan people get a super gross fetishized rap that *also* contributes to bi-erasure. First of all, bisexual/pan femmes who aren't on that full lesbian spectrum often get thought of as "red flags" as relationship candidates. Because, of course, we're just gay-cruising for attention. Even if we've been LOUDLY out even *before* they were. I had a late-in-life lesbian once thank me for my allyship. Ma'am, settle down. I recognize how valid you are! We don't need to gatekeep. That's what you learn the longer you're here. Once you move past the rainbows phase that we all do in our way, there's an awareness that our community is held together by love—by made-families. And that matters.

It matters because we're so fetishized and experience so much erasure that there are really not a lot of other narratives for bi/pan life other than the ones put on us by outsiders. If we even make it to a TV show, we're the promiscuous sidekick. If a once-straight, married politician gets caught with men in a sexual situation and tries to explain it away by saying, "I'm bisexual!" it continues these stereotypes that contribute to the harm and bi-erasure. Obviously, there are bisexuals who are in nonmonogamous relationships, and I am not here to say one thing or another; good for you, consenting adults. I'm happy you're happy. It takes a village to raise kids and afford a mortgage; carry on, poly-people!

But the number of times I have been invited as a third to a relationship or threesome is *many*. It happens all the time. Every time I say "I'm bi" out loud, the next sentence out of some guy's mouth is "Awesome, hey, are you into threesomes? I think I could talk my wife into it . . ."

Buddy, no.

It happens so often that I have to work into conversations early in relationships I plan to be out in that I'm into just my partner:

"Hey, so I really appreciate the invite to game night, but just so you know, Jay and I are in a monogamous relationship. LOL."

I know. But sometimes people *ghost*! And as an ADHD-er, I'd rather you find out now before I'm at your house because I don't always understand jokes or innuendo. Bisexuality is an attraction to all genders; different types of relationships are different kinds of relationships. You don't have to be in a throuple[41] to be a legitimate bi person. You can be. But that's a checkbox in the "majority narrative" imagination. You can also be me and married to someone nonbinary. Or whatever. The only true rule is you only have to roll your jeans above your ankle because your ankles get hot for reasons you don't truly understand. And of course you need to sit the completely inexplicable way you are currently sitting.

I know, how did I know?!

---

41 Three-person relationship.

People do what they do in relationships, but seriously, bi/pan people aren't alive sex dolls. Unless they say they are. Now you know too.

And also, let bi/pan men be. Every single time I talk to a bi/pan man, he is fighting against the straight idea that being into any man *at all* makes him fully gay. There are these clickbaity polls that go out on social media aimed at women titled "Would You Date A Bisexual Man?" that are specifically negative and harmful and perpetuate the idea that there are no bi/pan men.

Bisexual women just haven't met the right man, but all men who have sex with men are fully gay? Who do straight men think they are? Idris? Only Idris is Idris. Settle down, neckbeard.

When we, bi/pan people, meet each other in public, we just hug. Or wave to each other from our Subarus. *Thank God I don't have to explain myself to you for you to see I'm a person.* Or we announce ourselves in quieter ways like "Hey, does anyone need a drink or a snack or sunblock?"

We've been part of the queer community for all the time there has been a queer community. Stop the gatekeeping. We need you. Bisexuals have higher suicide rates than their lesbian/gay counterparts.[42] Trans+ folks are being murdered in unbelievably alarming numbers. People who would strip your rights away are the same ones who'll come for mine. We need to build knowledge, empathy, community, and coalitions. *Urgently.*

---

42   HRC staff, "Bisexual Health Awareness Month: Mental Health in the Bisexual Community," Human Rights Campaign, March 17, 2017, https://www.hrc.org/news/bisexual-health-awareness-month-mental-health-in-the-bisexual-community.

Mad Dog

And that was my life. All the way through high school. We were the same size by that point, so Karen was afraid to confront who I had physically become. She could no longer overpower me.

But that didn't mean she was finished with her ways. She just needed a new way to get to me, so she started using her alcoholic husband as a weapon instead. Every day, she'd wait until he got good and tight and then wind him up about whoever or whatever she wanted him to unleash his fury on.

It worked like a charm until, one day, she went too far.

Willy had come home from work already upset about something. Neil was home, which offered a certain amount of safety some of the time for me. When he was home, I would stay as close as I could to him, if possible. But that day when Willy got home, I was in the den, which was connected by a fireplace to the living room. They were in the living room: Karen, Neil, Ted, and Willy. Karen was winding Willy up about something Ted had done. Neil was sitting on the couch but trying to get her to shut up.

They were all arguing, which got my attention and brought me to the doorway.

Then everything started happening at once, seemingly in slow motion.

Willy grabbed my younger brother Ted and threw him into a blue curio cabinet. The glass shattered as he crumpled to the floor. Ted recovered quickly and looked around wildly, trying to figure out where the next attack would come from—from the ones who were supposed to love him.

He was crying, but angry.

"Stay away from me!" he warned Karen.

He warned Karen. She was the *threat*. And this child *knew* it.

But Karen wasn't done. This wasn't as bad as it could get. Yet.

"You're just making it worse for yourself!" Karen yelled back, *gleefully*.

Neil was in front of Willy trying to keep his father back, bodily. That gave my younger brother exactly the second he needed to find a weapon among the glass. He grabbed for a wicked shard, just as Willy got past Neil. Willy had his hands around my younger brother's throat pinning him to the ground with his drunken rage and mass.

Karen was trying to keep Neil away from them while Ted, silently, breathlessly, raised the shard and stabbed it into Willy's body, hitting him in the back of the leg.

Willy let out a roar of pain and reached for the glass sticking out of his leg. Blood spurted everywhere. He looked at the blade in his hand and then down at the gasping and terrified fifteen-year-old boy beneath him.

Neil leaped in front of Ted and put his whole body over my younger brother, covering him and screaming, "No!"

That got Karen involved. Not *her* baby. Her mad dog wasn't supposed to eat *her* baby.

Karen led Willy away to clean him up, and I listened to Neil speak soothingly to Ted, as Ted took huge gulping breaths.

"It's okay, bud. You did good. You're alive. It's over. He won't come at you again. You showed him."

Neil came over to me. We were alone.

Neil looked over at me sadly. Silent tears streamed down both our faces because we both knew what he'd said to Ted wasn't true. And that knowledge would cost Neil any normal life he might have had and would condemn him to be the failed protector *forever*.

I felt the wall behind me and slid down it, pulling my knees into my chest.

The Smiths had a couple of cops in the family and they had a few friends. So everything got taken care of like nothing had happened that night. Like always, lies were told and the paper disappeared. It's more common than you might think, especially in my little corner of suburbia. Maybe in yours too.

She Sent You to Him

Nothing holds people together like a shameful secret, and no one knew that as well as Karen did. She understood shame drove people to avoid being exposed. And everyone has *their* own things.

She didn't want you to love her. I mean, she did, I guess, to some degree. But what she *really* wanted was *mass adoration*. And the love of her children just didn't factor into that. Fear did.

And my need to love *a mother* to stabilize myself, to find my place in the world, gave her a way to control me. I was endlessly trying to earn her love.

Karen controlled with lies and fear. Except for her sons, whose power she wielded through manipulation whenever she saw fit. And, yes, I do mean "wielded," especially against their partners. So her sons' relationships with her had to be different. And boy were they.

It has often been remarked to me by wives and former wives of Karen's sons that Karen might have had more than a motherly relationship with her sons. An ex-wife noted to me that one of the things that grossed her out most about Karen's relationship with Will, her second son, was that she once caught them playing footsie under the table at dinner when her own foot was rubbed "sexually" by Karen's.

When she brought it up to Will, he got really defensive.

When we were still living at the Ranch (early nineties) with Karen, Will and Molly were living together at Karen's mother's house, the Homestead, where they had begun living upon her mother's death. These two homes were on two separate but adjoining streets. Karen would often show up at the Homestead unannounced, trying to start fights between Will and Molly, or trying to get Will to follow her home to beat up his father for any number of made-up reasons. We drove over there many times.

Something's Different

When I was sixteen, Karen started using me as a sexual lure for Will. I can say that now. I know what it was now. He was her "bad boy eighties" son, with a full, long hairdo and I want to say a Camaro, but I *really* don't know cars.

I suppose they kindly described Will as "incorrigible." Really, he was another narcissist who, like Karen, had become sexually abusive as a result of being sexually abused by the same man, Karen's stepfather. I know this because someone told me when I was still in the family.

Willy was devastated when he found out that Marie had been sexually abused by Karen's stepfather and begged for his daughter's forgiveness. He told me when he was drunk one time and I had to pick him up from the local watering hole. Marie told me the same story when I asked her about it. People knew, and I think that's the saddest part about people thinking they can wish family abuse away by not talking about it. People always *know*. Why they don't do anything is a question I can't answer. But I can tell you: they are just as guilty as the abuser if they are the ones telling the abused to keep quiet. *And they surely do tell them that.*

I started noticing something was different when I had to go visit Will more and she *really* cared how I looked when I saw him.

I was attending a semi-formal in tenth grade. I had to wear the dress she'd picked for me or I was on my own as far as paying for it. So I let her have her way: a blue halter sequin plunge for *my* boobs. I know. My sophomore year. *Way too much.* The disco ball dress.

She rushed me to be dressed by like 4 p.m., even though I didn't need to meet to take pictures until like 6 p.m. I needed everything to go normally.

Again, ADHD-ers do not love to be rushed for a secret and unknown timeline, so I remember this one pretty specifically.

Okay, so I'm dolled up[43] in the minivan and she hasn't explained where we are going, just vaguely referencing something about pictures. But we're heading toward downtown from almost all the way out in the town line, which is at least five miles, heading nearer to the school and kind of not a nearby errands distance.

"I'm meeting Mary at her house. I can't go to the school yet!" I said, alarm rising.

Please don't embarrass me. I've been allowed to have this one friend because she's part of a family you want to look good to.

Karen used to love not telling me where or why we were going to a place. She could see that it built anxiety in me that made me really easy to control and much easier to lie to.

After ten minutes, about a mile away from the high school, she turned left randomly onto a road that had only two elementary schools and a YMCA on it. I was out of guesses.

We pulled up to a softball field. Girls my foster sisters' age were playing. But my sisters were not there. We'd left them at home.

What?!

"Get out," she ordered.

"We're in the parking lot of a girl's softball game. Where am I going? I can't walk from here in these shoes . . ."

I spoke calmly, but I felt *wild* with anxiety.

This was a *very* naked dress to not know where you are or why you're there.

Karen sneered, and then, like it was just the most casual thing in the world, she said:

"Will wants to see how beautiful you look."

What the . . .

I let out a breath I didn't know I'd been holding.

---

43 I sure did say "dolled" on purpose. I just love Dolly. Rightly.

I looked around.

"Here?" I asked.

What I meant was: Why here? Why have you brought me to him? Why am I here?

"Yes. He's over there, next to Lolly," she said, smiling even more sweetly.

Great.

There he was next to his, I refuse to say hysterical, but let's call her an *extremely gaslit* baby mama, Lolly. Will and Karen, the "family narcissist squad," loved to trigger Lolly into super crazy-looking and hugely public outbursts. It was their way of making sure they collected (or, really, *created*) evidence they could use against Lolly in a future court proceeding because she was now pregnant with *their* child. A power move in Karen's mind where her son was concerned. *I know, I hear it.* They were both, mother and son, very calculating about gaining leverage for threats both real and imagined.

I got out of the sliding door minivan about as awkwardly as you might imagine and clunked across the field in my platform shoes, every inch the disproportionate child I was, heading over to meet Will and Lolly.

This was a softball game for Lolly's daughter, who was Becky and Chavonne's age, I realized. That's what we were all doing there, cheering for Lolly's daughter.

Will was surrounded by an entire bleacher of other parents, but I didn't see them. Lolly was crossing a softball field to meet me halfway, and I was focused on the growing rage on her face.

Great. She hates me. Why does she hate me?

When she got to me, she spoke.

"What are *you* doing *here*?" she whispered to me tersely.

She looked behind me, for Karen, I guessed.

"Sorry, Karen said Will wanted to take pictures with me or something, for semi-formal?" I said, stupidly gesturing to my stupid dress, like she didn't know I wasn't always dressed like a disco ball.

Dear God, why did I give in on the dress?

Lolly and I walked together in pregnant silence to the bleachers. Will sat smiling like a cat as I pulled up, and when we arrived at him, Lolly decided on her answer:

"I bet," she clipped.

"Don't be jealous, she's a kid," Will chided her, speaking for the first time.

"Do *you* know that?" Lolly retorted.

"What the f—k is *that* supposed to mean?!" he said.

Please, kill me now.

"I know you're f——g her! She came down here to show off for you!" she shrieked.

Oh my head. Any time, God!

I stood there in front of everyone, frozen in place, holding the stupid Marilyn skirt down lest it blow up.[44] Will grabbed me hard by the arm, and we traversed the field back to where Karen was parked. When we reached her, she got out to meet him.

"Doesn't she look beautiful?" she prompted. "*She* wanted to take a picture with you."

He slid a curious look at me while Karen let me know with her eye that I'd better not call her a liar.

"Then let's do it," he said. "I want to get back to the game."

We stood next to each other for photos, his enormous arm around my narrow, now much-too-naked shoulders.

Neither of them said anything else to me or each other about what Lolly had said. At least, I didn't hear them. We just finished the pictures and Karen and I got back in the van.

While Karen drove me away, she made me recount every single word she'd missed to the detail. Then, when I finally finished, she remained quiet for a long time.

"Good," she said finally.

---

44   Look, it wasn't the dress's fault that I was too young for it. Now that I'm grown I feel ready for the unwanted attention that dress brought. That's 100 percent a gross thing to have to protect against, but I would still look bad in it today.

When Lolly was first dating Will, she was married with two children. Will was also cheating on Molly, the mother of his toddler daughter. Those are facts. Lolly and her husband had two super gorgeous children and lived in a nice house in town. Her husband was cute and funny, so hopefully he was mean because he and Will were also "friends" at the time. Karen was super involved in the scandal. Will's daughter was maybe three or five max when this happened. When he left his baby mama, Molly, he fought her for every single inch in court during their long custody battle. But Karen was the one pushing the severity and toxicity of the fight. It defined her life. She was super litigious. Like every narcissist ever.

It took a while, but Will finally got visitation settled. However, on one of the very first times he was scheduled to visit, he had to work and left his toddler-aged daughter with Lolly. According to Karen, Lolly was so jealous of the baby and Will's love for her that she led the child into the street pretending she had lost Will's beloved dog, Mescal.[45] The child was nearly struck by a car. After that incident, the baby's mom raced back to court to strip him of his visitation when Lolly was around. Rightly.

I also know Lolly "wouldn't let him" pay his court-ordered child support, so I went with Karen on Wednesdays to and from Western Union to get a money order and then thirty minutes over to the local child support office where he could pay it and then reimburse Karen later. I read a lot in the car.

Whenever Will and Lolly had problems, which was often, I'd be treated like the adult I *surely was not* and was pulled in to help him do whatever sneaky thing he needed to do behind her back. They weren't married, which had something to do with him needing to keep his money away from her. Something about her being "pregnant" and "crazy."

For example, I was once tasked with helping him move out, a situation in which I did not want to be put, but Karen let me know I had no choice because I needed to help protect "The Family." Me, as a teenager. Not a lot to deal with physically yet. And with domestic violence situations being literally

---

45   I swear that was almost the dog's name.

the most dangerous situations even trained law enforcement face, I assume she intended to send me into harm's way. An acceptable loss.

When I was seventeen, Will and Lolly were in one of the "off again" phases of their relationship, and Will was staying on Karen's couch. I got home from work at 10 p.m. and Karen told me she was worried about him because he was sitting outside in his truck drinking beers. She wanted me to go outside and sit with him.

"I'm trusting you to make sure he doesn't drive," she said while ushering me outside and shutting the door behind me.

"I have homework," I said to no one as the door closed behind me.

It was October, dark, and cold. The grass was wet and I had short legs, so I bent down to roll up my jeans, shivering. My eyes searched the darkness for ghosts or skinwalkers.

These people.

I walked around the house and down the hill in the dark.

His truck was parked perpendicular to the house.

Okay, this is not how I go out . . .

Someone flipped on the floodlights, presumably Karen. Now with the backyard lit, I could see he was sitting in his truck. Alone. In the dark. Drinking beer. In the backyard.

Hiding. The truck was hiding behind the house.

His baby mama must be out looking for him. I sighed and opened the truck door.

"There you are!" he said cheerfully.

Expecting me. Great.

"What's up, bud?" I asked, not really listening to his response, more gauging how drunk he was.

"Ugh, Di . . ." he started.

Okay, very.

"You want a beer?" he offered.

"I'm seventeen," I said.

"Yeah, but like a mature seventeen," he said, putting out both of his hands and indicating my boobs. Seriously.

"I don't know what that is," I said.

I crossed my arms reflexively over my chest, trying to be smaller. He passed the beer to me again.

"I think you can handle it," he said, smiling as if this was known.

I took it from him and took a sip. I handed it back to him, immediately.

"No, thank you," I said.

I have ADHD. Trying new things isn't really a strength of mine.

"You don't like beer?" he laughed. "Then what do you drink?!"

"I'm seventeen," I said again, slower. People misunderstand me a lot.

"Right, right, keep your 'good girl' thing going," he said, apparently still laughing at a joke I didn't get.

What?!

"You're really beautiful, you know," he said, looking at the floor.

Please, no.

I tried to laugh it off. Because when a man gives you a compliment like that, as a woman, you get to judge instantly whether he is a safety risk. Especially as a trauma survivor. And if he is, you have seconds to calmly diffuse that situation. So you laugh at their inappropriateness, give them space to get out of it so they don't get their feelings hurt and don't beat you to death in response.[46] That's literally why.

Will leaned over and put his hands on me. It must have sent an electric shock through my body because I made it to the door in an instant.

Click. The truck's locks clicked into place.

"Now, listen . . ." he started, closing the distance I'd put between us.

I wasn't listening. I needed to get away. I didn't hear what he said. He might have said, "Now listen, I'm going to kiss you," but it was a shock to me when he grabbed me by my hair and stuck his hot and too-wide tongue in my mouth. He tasted like the beer I'd just tasted. Which had been my first beer, actually.

---

46 As Margaret Atwood famously observed: "Men are afraid that women will laugh at them. Women are afraid that men will kill them."

When he finally stopped, he let my hair go, and I was released.

"I have my period!" I blurted out as I found the door lock release. Finally escaping from the hot, sweaty truck and into the cold night air. Filling my lungs with huge gulps of air to supply the adrenaline hitting my legs.

And I *ran*.

She sent you to him, my inner voice reminded me.

She wasn't there when I came in. I ran up to my room and set sound traps along the steps. I lay awake for the entire night with that one thought ringing in my ears.

She sent you to him.

The next day when I saw her, I told her what had happened.

"So you didn't have sex with him?" she asked.

"No! I didn't have sex with *my brother*!" I shrieked.

"He's not your *real* brother," she said too calmly.

"I've thought of him as a brother since I was *seven*," I reminded her, thinking this made my point.

"Well, if *you* weren't such a sl—t, he wouldn't have thought he could get away with that. He was probably just testing you!"

"I'm a virgin," I said quizzically.

"Well, not a *real* virgin," she said.

She sent you to him.

The Wounded Knight

Much later, and after I was out of the house, a few peripheral family members came to me separately and asked whether I had ever felt like there was anything sexually inappropriate happening with Karen and her elder sons, specifically Will. As I look back, I can see why they asked. She had brought me to him as a sexual gift. As an apparently well-adjusted adult, I'll be honest: I don't know what some of the stuff going on was about, and I'm really hesitant to paint it with that brush from only my perspective.

That said, and this is important, most of the people involved in the day-to-day were at least *her* children, if not children themselves. I can't speak to their trauma; not because I don't know, but because it isn't okay for me to do so and I didn't blame them. Well, not all of them. I do blame the adult children or those who turned into abusers themselves. That's why I'm telling it I guess. I see a *choice*.

Neil was living in the home with us through his mid-twenties and was often teased for it. His older brothers said he was a mama's boy. When I was a teenager, I asked him why he stayed; he knew how awful things were, why not leave? He told me something I won't ever forget or ever stop being grateful for. He said:

"Who would protect you guys if I leave?"

I realized then that not everyone thought what was going on was okay, not everyone had been turning a blind eye, and maybe I'd been getting physically abused less as I had gotten older not only because *I had* gotten bigger, but because *he had*.

I hesitate to tell the next story because it isn't mine to tell, it's Neil's, but honestly, I really want to give some context to the absolute horror show that family was underneath the surface.

This happened when I was fourteen or fifteen, and Neil was twenty-one or twenty-two. The Smiths had a huge backyard and often hosted family cookouts. I remember Neil's old-fashioned (seventies) car was parked in the front yard, half-circle driveway. He and his older brother Will had gone into the car to talk about "things." No more than twenty minutes later, Neil punched through the windshield and had to go to the ER for stitches. No one knew what happened. At least, if they did, they didn't tell me.

But here's what happened after. Maybe a week later, Neil pulled up in his car, windshield fixed. He parked across the driveway purposely blocking everyone's cars. He and his then-girlfriend stormed into the house like a rage tornado. This wasn't normal for Neil; he was always the rational, anchoring force. Willy and Karen seemed to know exactly what this was about and scurried to make some sort of escape. But he had blocked them in. *He knew they'd try to run.*

Neil asked us kids to leave. When I saw his face, I knew at that moment what had been done.

There's this sound a voice makes when a human has been hurt in that way. And I can hear it. Maybe we all can. *A voice from hell.* It grates and chips someone's words as they leave the throat. People always seem surprised when they hear their own voices making that sound. It's because they don't talk about their pain. So the body isn't used to hearing it out loud, and it constricts the throat in fear. It strikes my heart in the same horrible way every time I hear it.

I *knew* I wanted to stay. I wanted to protect him from whoever had done this. I wanted to stand with him in his fight. Whomever it was with.

Willy told me to go to my room, but he said it so gently and so sadly, I felt like I was in a dream:

"Go up to your room, angel. Put everyone in their room first and keep them out of this room."

I nodded solemnly and took one last look at Neil, whom I had never before seen like this. He couldn't see me. He was crying, enraged, heartbroken, and devastated.

I was overwhelmed. Even in this world, there were things that happened and things that didn't. This didn't happen. No one stepped into Karen and Willy. Not like this.

From what I could gather, Will had been sexually abusing Neil at some point, on some level, and Neil found out in the car conversation the week before that his parents *had known.* He also knew they'd try to escape when he confronted them about it and that's what he was there to do.

Neil had been sexually abused. All the older kids had. And as a result of his abuse, Will had taken to sexually abusing the other siblings.

Neil and I became protectors after our abuse. Keith and Will went a different way.

As far as I can tell, abuse victims tend to react in one of two ways:

One: I had to go through it, so it's fine for you to go through it too. "I turned out fine."

Two: I had to go through this, so I will fight to make sure you never have to.

Not My Boyfriend

I started dating a little more earnestly immediately after Will forced his tongue down my throat. Maybe having a boyfriend would keep them away. Because patriarchy.

My first "boyfriend" lived across the street from me. We'd been friends first, so it felt like an extremely safe choice. We went from being friends who both didn't like gym class to friends who held hands at school. Karen immediately hated it and did everything she could to break us up. Once I was publicly dating, that meant there were more adults she needed to control, namely *his* parents (who were lovely). Though I didn't know this at first, Karen was scared of other adults finding out about her games, especially ones she considered "above her" socially. I ended up picking up on that pretty quickly, though.

But I want to tell you some of the stuff she tried.

I was seventeen and holding hands with my across-the-street neighbor who was not my boyfriend. He gave me his chain to remember him while I was traveling for winter guard competitions. (Mind your business! You want to write about your awkward high school relationships? No, you do not.)

Karen was so irritated, she snuck into my room and broke the chain. When I found the chain broken, she said I must have left it somewhere and "the dog" had chewed through the chain (that had clearly been pulled apart by someone with thumbs . . .).

I had to tell him it was broken. When I passed along Karen's excuse, being seventeen and still very much under her control, he thought I was lying. Because dogs would have chewed it. Of course.

Later, when he gave me a stuffed bear for Valentine's Day, she stole it out of my room and hid it, claiming I must've lost it because I'm so flighty.

This was what she did. She'd accuse me of losing something and then scream at and beat me about it. Then, I'd routinely find out *she'd taken the thing she'd beaten me for losing*.

I found the bear hidden in her room under a pile of junk she had piled in the baby crib that she had kept in her room since her youngest was born. Chavonne is seven years younger than me. I knew to look for it there because I'd found other things she'd hidden from me there that didn't belong to her after she sent me on errands to find something else for her.

And aren't people just the laziest when it comes to concealing dirty deeds from people they don't respect?

I took it back. She pretended she didn't know how it got there and then immediately installed *an alarm* on the door in her room.

"Because Di is a thief," she told everyone. And they believed her. Or they didn't. But either way, it was just *me*. Not worth the fight.

My not-boyfriend-friend once observed that the people in our house physically fought so much that coming over was like visiting "chicken fights."

Only after we were both adults did I tell him what had gone on in that house for real. He was the type of friend who never took anything I said seriously, and is still the same way. We've communicated almost exclusively through jokes and movie references for like twenty years.

After revealing the truth of what went on in that house, he said the only serious thing he has ever said to me:

"Di, I hope you know that you didn't deserve any of that, and, if I had known, I would've done something about it."

Kids who knew me didn't know. Huh.

"Thanks, dude," I said, shrugging.

"Seriously."

"I heard you."

We're still friends. We don't see each other enough because we both have kids. But we both hate how *Game of Thrones* ended and that's friends for life.

Careless

I've never told this story all the way through before because it's incredibly painful.

A lot of it is also missing from my memory. But I'm going to tell you about it because I think we need to talk about this.

When I was a teenager, the town held a really big fireworks display every year. They did it down at a huge park in the center of town. Hundreds of people attended. There were bands and ice cream and other food and snacks to make it fun. I usually had to scoop slush for my winter guard there too (because that's how we paid for trips). Unless your parents paid for your trips, or you somehow came up with the money yourself. Then winter guard ended up being a really intense after-school and weekends sport.

That year, I had signed up for an earlier shift because the Smiths had been invited to a friend's cookout across the street from the fireworks. I had brought my favorite outfit, eager to wander around the park and chat with other kids my age.

When I got to the party, I realized most of the people there were much older than me. Basically, it was adults who had kids, their kids (much younger than I was), and me, which was great because I wasn't really planning to hang out there.

"You need to stay and talk to people," Karen warned, "or you aren't going anywhere."

"I literally did the first shift in the heat so I could meet my friends!" I protested.

"You're not wandering around. Figure out where people are going, and then you can go," Karen said.

"Fine," I said.

She left, feeling satisfied about foiling my teenage plans.

I walked out to the front of the house where there were fewer people so that I could breathe.

Suddenly I felt someone behind me.

"You know, I can tell her I'll keep you safe, and we could walk over together," a new voice said to me.

I spun around in alarm, having expected the incoming person to be Karen to "finish our discussion" somewhere people couldn't hear.

"Oh," I said. "No, I'm good. She won't think you're less of a stranger."

"Moms love me," he said. "What are you drinking?"

"What, this?" I said, looking down at my red cup. "Sprite."

"Oh, no, you don't want that!" he said, grabbing my cup away and dumping it.

"I don't?" I asked.

"Yeah, hang on, I'll grab you what I brought!" he said.

I waited while surveying the park across the street for my friends.

I know . . . but I was seventeen and had no idea.

"I'm back!" he announced, as I looked up from my phone.

"Oh, hey! You're back!" I repeated. Because ADHD.

"Yeah, here you go!" he said, handing me back my cup.

I took it from him.

Again . . . I know. But who would have cared enough to warn me?

"What's this?" I asked, looking into the cup.

"It tastes just like a Jolly Rancher," he replied, confidently.

I took a sip.

"Not bad," I said. "A little sour."

"It's sour apple pucker," he said. "I thought all girls loved it."

I scrunched my face. *All girls.*

"Well, thanks, but I don't drink," I said, trying to hand it back to him.

He put his hands up to refuse it.

"Might as well finish it. I can't pour it back in the bottle," he said.

"Well, I'm seventeen. Can't you finish it?" I asked.

"I'm twenty-four, and no, I can't. I don't drink that girly stuff. My girlfriend does," he said.

Whew, a girlfriend. He isn't trying to date me.

"Okay," I said, finishing the drink.

I did not make it to see my friends that night.

It's hazy how I got to where I was, but I remember him being on top of me. I tried to push him off, but all my body parts felt off their tracks.

"Stop," I said, managing to move my mouth.

"I'm almost finished," he answered, laughing.

Laughing at me.

And then I just didn't fight.

I looked up at the sky beyond him, backlit by the fireworks exploding across the smoke-filled inky black background. While he grunted and laughed, I lay in the dirt with tears streaming silently down the sides of my face.

When he was done, he let me go and then disappeared.

I didn't leave at first. I just stared at the sky for what felt like an eternity.

Eventually I got up, barefoot and disheveled, and tried to walk back to the party. I had no idea where I was. The fireworks must've been over because hundreds of people were walking at me while I was trying to fight the crowd in the other direction.

I could feel the mess and blood of what he had done running down my thigh and closed my eyes to fight the sob from escaping into this many people.

I stumbled.

Suddenly a teenager I didn't know very well came to my aid, holding me up as I tried to keep going. His name was John. He played sports. I played softball but did mostly artsy stuff. I didn't know he knew me.

"Di?" he said. "Are you okay?"

"I don't think I am," I responded. "I'm hurt and I'm lost. Do you know where I am?"

"No, I don't because I'm still messed up," he answered. "For the fireworks?" He indicated the sky above.

"Okay, well, can you take me back to the park?" I asked.

"YES!" he said. "I just came from the park!"

"Excellent," I said, and we gingerly walked each other back. Karen stood outside her car waiting for me. Fuming.

"Thanks, dude," I murmured. "Do you need a ride back?"

"No. I'm good now. I've got it," he replied.

Karen at least waited for him to be out of earshot before unleashing whatever she had been holding back, blessedly. While I did not know this kid well, I didn't want him to hate me either. This totally random angel.

"Where have you been? We were waiting!" she hissed.

"I fell, I'm sorry. Can we go?" I said, limping to not feel the blood.

That's all I remember of that night, and I don't want to think too hard about it.

A few days later, Karen got a phone call. It was the person who had hosted the Fourth of July party. After she'd hung up, she came to talk to me. Softly, so clearly building toward a big manipulation.

"Di," she began, taking a deep breath. "That was HomeOwner on the phone . . ."

My heart stopped beating while I waited for her to finish. Afraid to move. Afraid for it to be real.

". . . one of her neighbors found a hat in their backyard that didn't belong to them that had a phone number in it. When they called that number to give the hat back, it was HomeOwner's house. She's worried because she used to have a stalker in high school and thought it might be his."

"Okay," I said, carefully.

"Well, someone mentioned they saw you there. Do you remember who you were . . . *there* with?"

Crap.

"Um, yes, you can probably let her know that she shouldn't be afraid. I was there with her cousin, so he wouldn't hurt her," I said. *Probably.*

"Which cousin?!" she squawked.

"I don't know, I think his name was Mack?"

"You think?"

"I don't really remember everything about that night."

"Were you drinking?!"

"Not really," I said. "Half a cup of mostly sprite, I think?"

She spun away and got back on the phone with HomeOwner. She whispered the entire call. I tried to listen, but also I didn't want to hear. Dueling priorities.

When she found me in the Princess Prison, I was lying on the rug. She sat and leaned in conspiratorially:

"HomeOwner's twenty-four-year-old cousin, *Mack*, is engaged, and the family, a big family in the community, would like to keep it quiet from *the fiancé's* family," she said. "I promised them you would never tell anyone."

His family didn't want the more prominent family he was marrying into to know what he'd done. And *his* family was willing to demand that of me. Who was I, I guess?

"Why would I want to tell anyone?" I said.

"Well, you wouldn't," she said.

She patted me on the knee as she carefully exited the Princess Prison. I was her ally now. Part of keeping family secrets secret. I bore the weight of that alone so that I never had to say these words:

I was raped at a family party by a family friend. My "family" covered it up.

Tragically, that isn't where this story ends.

Because soon my period was late.

There is no way to accurately put into words the shattering effect that slightly positive pregnancy test had on my ability to function. I just could not fathom it. I couldn't pretend it hadn't happened anymore.

"I think I'm pregnant," I told Karen later that day when I worked up the courage. I didn't wait because I felt contaminated by him. I felt like he had stolen all my dreams. He hadn't just raped a teenage girl at a party, and he had done so without using a condom. He had planned enough to bring drugs for someone, but not a condom.

"You think?!" Karen shrieked, whirling around to face me.

I was pacing.

"No, I am. I took a test, I know I am," I said. Nothing to lose at this point. *Maybe she would kill me.*

She sat in stunned silence for what felt like five minutes while I paced the bathroom like a trapped tiger.

Finally, she spoke.

"Is it . . . is it, from *that* night?"

"Yes! Obviously!" I shrieked.

"Get the phone book," she said.

"The what?" I said, spinning.

"Get the phone book off the attic stairs and call the clinics," she instructed.

I went to the attic, took the phone book off the step, looked up "clinics," and found nothing.

"What kind of clinic?" I asked her.

She looked at me incredulously, and then lowered her voice, hissing: "*Abortion* clinics! You idiot!"

"I am seven*teen* years old," I said, enunciating meaningfully on teen.

She had me call every single clinic with a phone number that was within driving distance. A lot of them were different numbers and names for the same place:

"Honey," one nurse finally told me, "you just called me on the other line, and this isn't a situation you want to be price shopping in. Call me back if you want to make an appointment."

"What an idiot," Karen said when I told her what the nurse had said. "Get dressed, we're going for a drive."

It was raining hard. I remember the water streaming and the sound of the windshield wipers. One of them wasn't working as efficiently as it should be, and it really bothered my ADHD. She drove to a nearby playground and parked in the middle of the parking lot. No one would be there in the rain. She had chosen her stage well.

"You're getting an abortion," she finally said.

I didn't say anything. I was totally numb. I felt completely hollow. Like someone had put a life-killing toxin in me, and every breath I took, it spread. I experienced a complete brain/body separation. I existed entirely in my mind, imagining if I felt my body, I would feel the crime scene boarded up within me.

"But I am a Catholic," Karen said. "So if I'm going to help you get out of this, we're going to have a serious conversation about your sexual experiences."

I snorted.

"There isn't anything to tell," I said.

"Well, clearly there is, and I'm not having my family go through the embarrassment of *another* teenage pregnancy *for you*! I'm a good mother!" she said.

I didn't answer.

"This is *your own* fault!" she accused.

She continued to ask a barrage of incredibly personal and totally inappropriate sexual questions, and remember: this woman is not my mother. What sexual positions had I tried? What sexual things had I done? Every sexual contact story, consensual or not. She made me retell the stories back to her. Both rapes. Then and now.

Finally she said, "I'm convinced you're worth helping, but you are going to pay me back the money for this; we shouldn't have to be out *family money* because of your carelessness."

My carelessness.

Finally she drove us home and we made the appointment. Unfortunately, at the time I called, I was only a little more than four weeks late, and you needed to be six then for there to be enough cells for a procedure to even be possible.

Karen drove me to a nearby clinic, muttering the entire time that I had better have a good excuse ready if we were to see anyone she knew there.

"What would they be doing there, if not the same thing?" I asked.

"Working!" she hissed.

They had to put me out for the procedure, and when I woke up, Karen was in the room with me.

I was in a wheelchair with a bowl in my lap, and I was shaking from head to toe from the anesthesia. I was also very cold, dressed only in a thin hospital gown, all the while trying to understand why all this had happened to me and wondering whether Mack had already hurt someone else.

She cleared her throat to speak and I looked up.

"Let's never do this again," she said jokingly.

I looked at her incredulously and then threw up.

I promised I would never tell this story, and I carry so much shame for every minute of what happened to me.

But as I've grown and tried to heal into adulthood, I wouldn't want this for my friends, my daughter, or anyone else. This wasn't my fault. Mack was a predator. If it hadn't been me, it would've been someone else. Someone else's daughter.

And I could survive this.

It's 2022 as I sit down to write the story I thought I'd never tell, and I wonder whether I should delete this section and fly under the radar.

Roe v. Wade has been overturned and, just yesterday, I wrote an email to my daughter to read in the future detailing my pain and my frustration at what's happening.

But I have listened to this debate, and I have been shamed into silence by my regret over the rape itself for almost twenty years now, while people running for office tell newspapers that "children should find healing carrying their rapist's child to term." I realize I am responsible for my daughter coming into her full adult power, and in order for me to do that with any authenticity, I'm going to need to be honest. Even though it scares me. Even though I'm not done dealing with it yet. Maybe I won't ever be.

I live in Massachusetts. My rights have not changed. As long as my daughter, Artemis, doesn't leave here, her rights have not changed. But that's nowhere near good enough. It would not have been good enough for Ruth Bader Ginsberg, and it's not good enough for me. And I'm a writer, apparently, so let's get into it.

I do not have regrets about having an abortion. I'm grateful I had the choice to wait and bring my children into the world with all the love and care I could provide as a mother. I'm grateful to the medical professionals who help women and pregnant people make impossible and often heartbreaking choices every day.

But *I* didn't choose this. *Mack did.*

My story is heartbreakingly common. We teach kids to be wary of strangers while, in fact, most kids are assaulted or raped by a family member or family friend. Like I was. There will be more little girls raped in the dirt by adult men in small towns who feel untouchable. I won't be the last. And politicians will protect them because some of them are guilty of crimes against women and children themselves. Every accusation is a confession.

But from my position, I regularly wonder why this debate is framed the way it is. I've never known anyone to be "pro-abortion." Most people know someone who has needed abortion services. One in four women will be sexually assaulted. About half of the women I know have needed abortion healthcare. Their reasons are as varied as they are common.

But they were all serious about why they sought abortion services. No one had "used it as birth control" or could've "just kept their legs closed," or any other gross narrative I've heard bandied about lately.

Adoption was not an option in my case because, as I mentioned, this twenty-four-year-old man had a semi-powerful family in my small town, and my status was not secure as an "underage" foster kid. *I had no rights.* Your child is automatically in foster care if you are a foster kid, and it isn't like they keep you with them either. I knew what monsters lived in the foster care system.

There wasn't an option for me to adopt out the cells either. I would have to grow my rapist's thoughtless crime into a child who would automatically go to foster care. Or he'd get custody. My rapist. That's the dirty little secret of the "adoption" narrative, especially since they've been saying the Quiet Part out loud lately. And the Supreme Court just told everyone the goal was to raise the "domestic supply of infants."

So the next time you hear someone shouting down abortion in a particularly demeaning way to women, I want you to think they're talking about me. And act like a human. *Please.* Because a woman shouldn't need to be someone's mother, sister, or friend to be worthy of human dignity and bodily autonomy. I am all of those things, but I'm a person too. *I'm someone on my own.* And so are you.

The Tape Recorder

When I was eighteen or so, Karen sat me down to tell me she had some terrible news to share. She told me my partner at the time had told their friends about some of our private moments together.

"I ran into Suzie, Mindy's mom, and she told me everything. I guess all your friends were laughing at you, and Suzie felt like someone should tell you," she said. "Even *your* type of people can't want your business all over town."

"Okay, Karen," I responded. She lied to me all the time. It was like breathing for her, and I'd learned not to trust her. When I started to walk away, she continued.

"Actually, she told me *all about it* . . ." she reported gleefully and went on to tell an extremely private story that no one but me and one other person should know.

I felt the air leave my lungs as I sank to the ground.

"How did she . . ." I couldn't think. I couldn't breathe. Someone I loved and trusted had betrayed me and, apparently, so many people in our small town knew that it had gotten back to my mortal enemy. And now Karen could use it against me.

I cried for a week and didn't respond to any calls or outreach from my obviously former partner or former friend, both of whom had betrayed me.

Karen took all the calls.

Just like she wanted.

Maybe a year or so after this, I was dating this guy, Todd.[47] Todd felt like he was above Karen, and he let her know it, regularly. We were in a long-distance relationship because he was away at college, so I was on the phone with him *a lot*.

One day I heard the landline phone ringing after a few rings, so I had to run to answer the call and take it in a different room than usual to avoid his call going to voice mail. As I ran through the dining room, Karen noticed and came running up behind me.

"I've got it," I said to her. "It's for me."

She stood behind me, too close, with a curious look on her face.

"What's wrong?" Todd asked on the phone.

"Nothing, hang on," I said as I covered the mouthpiece and turned to Karen.

"What?" I asked her.

"You don't take phone calls in here," she answered cryptically.

"I what??" I asked, trying to make sense of what was happening.

"Take it in the living room," she said.

"What? No. Why? They're watching TV there," I said.

"Di, I have class. What's happening?" Todd asked impatiently.

"What? Nothing. She's leaving. Hang on," I said, uncovering the phone.

Karen went into the kitchen, the next room, looking back hesitantly.

Maybe she doesn't want me to read her mail? I thought, looking at the piles of envelopes thrown all over the dining room table and chairs. She didn't open most of it or deal with it. She mostly collected it, sorted it in piles, and screened anything that came for me, especially important mail that she'd told me never came. When I tried to get a driver's license, it had to be sent out many times because "it just didn't get here." Really, she was taking it and hiding it every time they sent it. I eventually found the letters hiding, opened, behind the driver's side visor of *her* car.

Maybe she was worried I'd find another important document she'd hidden?

---

47 Another narcissist whom you will remember as the kid who puked when I told him I'd been raped as a child.

I sat on the floor and chatted with Todd about his day. While my ADHD brain was sitting still, I started fidgeting with everything in touching distance. I felt something smooth under the heating register paneling close to the floor.

What the . . .

I pulled the item out.

It was a tiny tape recorder.

I looked down at my hand, instantly realizing *this* was what she hadn't wanted me to find. Curious to see what she had been recording, I pressed rewind, then play, and instantly felt sick, dizzy, and betrayed as I heard my own voice talking to Todd on the phone. I stood up too fast.

Karen came around the corner fast, but not fast enough.

"What is this?" I asked.

"Nothing!" she said, grabbing for my hand.

"What?!" Todd said. "Di, what's happening?!"

"Karen has been recording all our phone calls," I said, more to myself than him.

"WHAT?!" he bellowed.

She snatched the device from my open hand and stormed off.

"What the h—l, Di?" Todd said. "I've gotta go. Are you okay?"

"Bye," I said and hung up.

But my mind was racing. This was how Karen knew. None of my friends had betrayed me. No one had lied. There was no grand conspiracy in which everyone hated me. If there were, Karen had created it. There was no inherent thing in me that had caused all of this anguish in my life. That made me unworthy. There was a tape recorder.

And a monster who wanted to destroy me.

Hoarders

Karen is a hoarder.

The mail wasn't an isolated situation.

After her mother died, Karen wouldn't let any of her mother's possessions go. So anything that was in the basement stayed where it was, and everything of her mother's from the upstairs got brought down to "the Gym."

Her mother had apparently owned some sort of in-home salon and work-out studio for women. Downstairs had changing stalls in the hallway beside the furnace room. I remember there was gross reddish maroon carpeting from the hallway through the Gym. There were also dead mice everywhere in various states of decomposition.

Junk filled the Gym from floor to ceiling. I don't mean *a lot* of junk. I mean literally there was discarded stuff in the room from the floor to the ceiling. And it was a *huge* room. There was so much garbage that there was only a small foot traffic path between the hallway and Willy's downstairs office, which was also half filled to the ceiling with overflow junk from the Gym. I thought this was totally normal and often asked friends where their junk room was when I'd visit for the first time. Today, I can't keep anything. I donate everything I haven't used in a year.

The Smiths' bedroom was also filled with junk. An air hockey table they had intended to use was covered on top and below with clothes and garbage.

A crib that their youngest daughter had used was also filled with clothes and garbage. Everywhere that wasn't a pathway was covered in clothes and garbage. When I was a teenager, Willy moved to the downstairs "apartment" after Keith moved out of it.

There's an "apartment" downstairs in the finished basement because there's always an adult Karen raised in a bad relationship where an extra sleeping arrangement is needed in an emergency. It's been that way since Keith and Peggy got divorced over twenty years ago. Apparently, Becky lives there now with her boyfriend. Neil lived there for a while too.

The downstairs laundry room was outside of the apartment, closest to the Gym, and filled with a mountain of dirty clothes. Willy would rage about it because it was overflowing with dirty clothes and shared space with the furnace room, right beside the oil furnace. It was a fire hazard. Every Saturday, I would have to go downstairs and sort and fold everyone's dirty laundry from the house. I would sit on the mountain of dirty clothes, sort by owner, and fold. Dirty clothes. People, usually Mae or Neil, would come down and ask what I was doing.

"Folding the clothes," I'd say, matter-of-factly.

"You're folding the *dirty* clothes?" they'd ask.

"Right, so mom can wash them," I'd answer. I didn't think there was anything wrong with this.

"How long have you been doing this?" they'd ask.

"All day," I'd say.

"Why don't you just wash them, so you don't have to do this every week?" they'd ask.

"She won't let me wash them. She says I need to sort and fold them for her so *she* can wash them."

"But then she doesn't wash them?" they'd ask.

"I guess not," I'd respond.

Karen basically made piles upstairs of the laundry, then she'd have me throw all the laundry in the laundry room, and then I'd stay downstairs all day sorting and folding it on the weekends. Then she'd just buy more clothes.

Sometimes I was allowed to bring my boom box with me, so I didn't mind so much. I listened to the radio a lot. I usually snuck a book. Away from Karen was okay with me.

The Homestead is also a ranch-style house from the front. The house went down a hill in the back, so it actually had a second level that was entirely furnished. There was an in-ground pool put in when I was around fourteen, although I was never ever allowed to swim in it. Not a single time. From the time I moved in with the Smiths, I had chores. It was just a way to make sure I couldn't go out and play or read or talk to anyone. I didn't have any friends, and when people would invite me to things out of sympathy, or because they'd invited the whole class, she'd pull a full-blown Wicked Stepmother and make lists of things I'd have to do if I wanted to attend. I almost *never* got through them.

But one time I did get through them and I got to go to a neighbor's birthday party at the town's roller skating rink. I was eight years old. Lindsey was a nice girl with good parents who lived nearby. Karen wouldn't buy a present for me to give her, so I gave her my most treasured possession: two coupons for free breakfast cereal. I gave them to Lindsey's mom and went out and skated, feeling normal for once. Some of the kids weren't nice to me, but I didn't care. I was a normal kid for those couple of hours.

A few weeks later, I received a package in the mail with my free cereals in them. Lindsey's mom had sent away for the cereals and gave them my address. I was extremely touched.

When I started having performances for band, chorus, and other artsy things for high school later, Lindsey's parents would drive me. The Smiths never came to anything I did that their "real" daughters didn't do as well, so this was really my only way to participate in other activities. Lindsey's parents would often ask on the way home whether I wanted to go out to dinner with them, too, but I always felt like I was intruding. They never made me feel that way. They were genuinely kind people, but I felt like an alien when I saw normal kids with their normal parents . . . you know, parents who wanted to be involved with them and cared about what they were up to.

Not like the Smiths.

Chores

The three front rooms of the Homestead where visitors would go were the family room, which was at the entrance and acted like a front room or parlor; the kitchen; and the den, which had a second TV in it and acted more like a family room. The house had three bedrooms. The girls shared, the boys shared, the parents had one, and I was in the Princess Prison. One good thing about the Princess Prison was I could hear Karen walking up the stairs whenever she was coming.

But every room in the house was my responsibility. I had to get up early and finish a list of daily chores before school. Whatever I couldn't finish, I'd have to finish after school. I also had additional weekly chores to do on the weekends. And then on Sunday, whenever I finished my weekend chores, I had a "big project" to finish before I could do anything I wanted to do. The "big project" was usually sorting some type of endless pile of junk, such as the laundry room, the attic, her bedroom, the girls' bedroom, or the Gym—some task that was just intended to take up the remainder of any playtime I might try to enjoy.

And on and on that went. If I didn't have homework to finish after chores, I'd stay up all night reading.

Once, when I was about nine, the Smiths had a New Year's Eve party. I told Karen that if she let me stay up late with them, I would get up early and clean up from the party.

"I promise," I said.

Well, because I stayed up so late, I didn't wake up until after Karen and broke my promise. When she woke up before me, she came in to wake me. I was wearing my *Babysitter's Club* nightgown. I remember because she tore it off me. My Nana Santos had given it to me. It was one of the only things I had from my family.

I got to the family room, and we both surveyed the mess. She was so angry she grabbed me by the face and pulled both my cheeks away from my mouth in opposite directions. I called this move "pinching my cheeks." It hurt so much, and she did it all the time because it would cause my lips to split and bleed like crazy. I guess that's what she wanted.

This time, however, she didn't stop there. She threw me on the couch by my face. I landed on my back, and she lunged at me. She choked me around the throat with her hands, placed her enormous knee on my chest, and pinned me there while I clawed at her fingers and tried to escape until I passed out. She could have *easily* killed me. My life would've been over because I broke a promise to get up early and clean her house after a party when I was nine.

When I got older, my chores stayed the same, but because of my school, sports, and work schedules, I had to pack them into my "free" time. Chores were to take place before homework, and if I didn't want to be shamed when I got to school for not having my homework done, I had to stay up past midnight every night to finish. And I still didn't always finish. The teachers just thought I was a bad kid when I was falling asleep in class. When they'd call her on the phone to talk about my performance, she'd pretend I had all the time in the world and must just not be applying myself, or she'd say it was because I had been in foster care, but she'd adopted me.

"What a good mother," they'd all agree.

One time, she even came into the school to sit at the desks while the other kids were there to demonstrate she was a good mother who cared about me finishing my work. I was in ninth grade, and she sat there while I finished the homework I'd gotten behind on for the week. I had a job, multiple traveling sports teams I had to be on, and responsibilities at home. But she needed to play mother of the year.

The science teacher/pedophile that I mentioned earlier who had to marry one of his students looked up at me doing my work. Karen was sitting beside me, and I was praying to die and burning from shame while all the kids looked on and whispered about what was happening.

"Good for you, Mom," the science teacher/pedophile said to Karen.

That's all she needed. She got the dopamine hit she wanted, and he thought she was a great mother. The pedophile who's lucky I'm not revealing his name. And she told *everyone* that story. She dined out on the pedophile's praise for the rest of the time I lived there.

In reality, she was scheduling more and more things for me to do to meet her growing vicarious living needs: keeping some areas of her house clean so people thought she was a good wife, being a sports mom so people could observe her being a good and involved mother, and having enough money weekly to buy more clothes and junk. Where did you think all the junk piles came from? Not from a landscaper with five kids living at home. Disposable income. I was giving her all the money I made at after-school and weekend jobs. All she did all day was shop.

And not just shops either. She'd go to Marshalls. Marshalls is like a T.J. Maxx. Every Marshalls within driving distance, she'd spend hours shopping and then put everything on layaway. But she only picked up about 25 percent of the items. She just left the rest on layaway. Often, I'd have to call the store and ask for an extension on orders she had no intent of ever picking up.

When I was in my twenties and living in Atlanta, I reached out to check in on Karen. One of her children reported to me that the hoarding had gotten worse and she had been saving her *used* toilet paper. The paper she used to wipe herself. I haven't asked anyone about anything since. But I suspect the situation hasn't improved as she's gotten older and more infirm. She's in her seventies now, as a friend of hers often reminds me.

No one could protect me when I was a child, or Marie for that matter, but folks have real strong opinions on what a child should reveal about *their own* abusive childhood.

Folks always protect the abuser because they're the ones who will play the victim. I don't play the *victim*. I play the *survivor*. That's how you can tell the difference.

Dirty Water

For the uninitiated, when you are born in the Boston area, they stamp a culture onto your soul that inspires movies. About gangsters. Where pedophiles just kind of disappear and meh. Life, eh?

So here's what you need to know: There are definitely sections of Boston that are old money, came-over-on-the-Mayflower-already-set kind of money. Kennedy money. They do live in Boston; they also live up and down the coast of Massachusetts in mansions that overlook the glorious Atlantic ocean. Boston Brahmins. And while maybe they would say that they are what defines Boston culture, we, Boston's immigrant poor, would disagree.

Boston is a coastal city with history dating back over 250 years. In Massachusetts public schools, which are incidentally some of the best in the nation, we have our history drummed into us. We're taught that Massachusetts was one of the first colonies, that we are a nation of immigrants,[48] that we are the ones who always stayed true to our better angels through geniuses like John Adams. This heavily glossed history gets a little more critical when we are old enough, but *not a lot more* if you catch my drift.

We're taught that our ancestors fought to free enslaved people in the Civil War and then when enslaved people ran North to freedom, our communities

---

48   No one's grandparents are from here. I mean, statistically yes, but anecdotally? No.

here welcomed them.[49] Those of us who are also Irish are taught that we came over in droves during the Great Potato Famine and that we were starving in the streets when they sent us off to fight in their Civil War or to build their railroads. To death.

We all knew the pretty stories they told us about enslaved people were half-truths because the stories they told about the Irish were. Oh, and while I'm here not writing an entire book with fake stories we students get (or at least got) here about the colonist's relationship with First Nations people, it's called Massachusetts. That's not for "Bob Massachusetts," y'all. That acknowledged always-partially-fake history mixed with basically every kind of immigrant culture informs Boston's mosaic, but also notoriously racist,[50] reputation.

Our general attitude is not improved by the terrible weather half the year. But our sports teams are usually pretty great. I hear. I don't watch. And, obviously, we have a lot of the best colleges and universities in our own backyard. And in those ways, it was really cool to be from here.

While this area is famously known for witches and the much-too-late mea culpa that led to our seriousness about religious liberties and mass hysteria, it's also heavily Catholic. But not as Catholic as it once was.

If you saw the movie *Spotlight* about the *Globe* reporters, that was a true story[51] about this area. If you didn't read the article or catch the movie, it's the story of how Boston-area Catholic priests who were known to be pedophiles and abusers of children in their flock were moved around by the Church. The scandal rocked this community hard and made a lot of people question their participation in the Church. The parishioners felt betrayed.

I acknowledge that this shared trauma changed how we view the Church here. My experience in the Church happened before this news broke, but not before the whispers about the stories or the priests. Hindsight contextualizes my lens on these stories. I acknowledge that.

---

49   Continues heavy glossing that ignores Boston's actual history . . .
50   I know! I couldn't keep it nice, huh? Other people are here; they know I know.
51   Michael Rezendez, "Church Allowed Abuse by Priest for Years," *Boston Globe*, January 6, 2002, https://www.bostonglobe.com/news/special-reports/2002/01/06/church-allowed-abuse-priest-for-years/cSHfGkTIrAT25qKGvBuDNM/story.html.

In order to be married in a Catholic Church, you have to go through a series of indoctrinating rituals that are called "sacraments." You do your First Communion, which is when you have your first confession. Kids are usually younger for this. I was eleven.

When I went in for my first confession, which is a prerequisite to receiving Communion, I must have missed a direction somewhere. I said the whole spiel I was supposed to say and then there was total silence. In my anxiety, I just started prattling away like I do, and the priest just sat there silent.

Unsure what to do, I started "confessing harder," thinking he didn't believe me that I was sorry for kicking my brother, when I heard the priest say to someone else:

"I'm so sorry. I have to interrupt you. I have someone confessing over here to a closed door."

Then he opened the slider and said, "Please wait your turn."

Perfect.

When he came back to me, I literally lied about what my sins were just so I could get out of there faster. Whatever. God heard me the first time.

When I was sixteen, two years before the Spotlight story came out, I was going through the last sort of "school-aged" sacrament, confirmation. This one is where you are accepted into the community as a "full" Catholic. But before we were able to complete that step, we had to go on a retreat with the priest, Father Priest. Father Priest is pretty well known for his pro-equal marriage sermons that he was giving before others had started doing so. The parents thought he was very good looking. They called him "Father What-A-Waste." Sorry, Father.

Father Priest had gone to all of our parents in advance of this trip to get them to write letters to us. The idea of this exercise was for us to sit around a campfire reading these in front of each other.

While we were around the campfire, Father Priest was saying very lovely things about how "our parents' love for us is like God's love for us."

I felt panic building in me about what I was going to say when he didn't hand me a letter. How would the other kids react to me being there with them, so unwanted?

Father Priest sensed I was in distress and approached.

"Everything okay, Diana?" he asked.

He called me by my name. I think he liked saying it. He had been engaged to a lady named Diana, whom he left when he heard the "call" from God. *He told me.* People share whatever their thing is with me. Always.

"Yes . . . Did my foster mother not write a letter?"

"She did write you a letter," he said. "She wrote you *the best* letter!"

She did?

He handed it to me, already opened.

"You should have a little more faith in people's ability to love you," he said.

I looked down at the four-page letter in my hand.

She had numbered it.

"Well, I'll leave you to it!" Father Priest said.

She wrote me a note?

It was folded up in my hand. I was almost scared to read it. I figured it would just say "hahahahahahaha" for four pages. But it didn't. I've kept the letter she wrote for me to read in front of everyone, all these years since, in a shoebox full of all the cards I've ever gotten from people since I was a teenager. This is what it said:

Feb 26th, 1999

Dear Diana,

I consider you our chosen child. I remember the date you arrived very well. Do you? February 4th 1990. You arrived at 4:45pm just before supper. You had on blue pants and a yellow shirt. Your hair was in a LONG ponytail. The first thing you said to us was a big "Hi! My name is Diana! What's yours?" My first thought was "what a pretty little girl." I finally had a little girl with LONG hair.

You were cute as a button and so small. You acted so brave and tough, but inside you were so scared. I bet you didn't think I saw through you like that.

You had all kinds of questions, and still do. That has not changed. I couldn't wait to dress you in a little dress with ribbons and bows. When you told us your birthday was coming soon, and told us the date. A flash went through my head about my past, and a question went into my mind. Could this be a second chance? Maybe you did not know this, but I lost two babies after Neil, and one would have been due in March around your birthday!

I remember thinking how lucky and blessed I felt. I told Dad, and he said that I was right! So, by you being given to us, only made you more special to me. The longer we had you only made me think that God could not correct the problem with the baby I carried inside of me, so it took it back up to Heaven and made it stronger and then had someone deliver you to us in a different way. It does not matter how God delivers his children to us. It only matters that we were given the second chance to have you, and for that I feel thankful. Do you? I have always kept this secret in my heart, waiting for the right time to tell you: I love you!

We have watched you grow day by day from a small, little, funny, little, puffy puss with big brown eyes into a beautiful shapely young lady. I am so happy to have the chance to mold you and shape you to be what you are. I am sorry for any time you were not happy. We have had our little ups and downs but we always have come through them together.

We have enjoyed the many special moments together holidays, birthday, vacations and many more. The most special to me are the ones when it is just you and me. When I have a chance to enjoy the same little girl with the funny face and her cute little wit that makes me laugh. I hope you always keep that. Life can change so many things. I hope we always stay close and can manage to steal some time for our one to one. I enjoy them, and they are special to me.

Always remember you are not just our child, but a special child chosen from God and given to us in a special way by Him. We love you very much and I hope we will always be close. I believe and I know you do too that all things happen for a reason. Sometimes I know this is hard to keep in mind. God works in funny ways, and maybe what happened this weekend happened for a reason. Maybe that was to prove to you how much we do love you. Also that there was a lesson to be learned from it and that is that honesty is the best policy. Diana, you have a lot to offer in life, and are a very giving person. With some guidance and direction, you will be okay. I knew that not long after you came. That was when you said "I did it! I did it!" and I said "what did you do?" and you said to me "I finally kissed Neil!" I knew then that you belonged to us and you were strong and you were going to be okay.

Well, I'm sure you are tired of reading, and they say absence makes the heart grow fonder. Here comes a random statement; you are never tired of reading so I guess I'll have to say I am tired of writing. But there are so many things I have memories of but I'll save them for another time. A special time. Do you realize this is the longest you have been away from us, not with family? We miss you so let's do this like we did when you were little. You can think of us every night at ten and we will think of you, that way we will always be close even though you are away. We love you.
Love, Mom and Dad.

Ps: Don't forget ten o'clock . . .

I have no idea what she's talking about.

Literally.

From the "molding and shaping" to the funny face and hot body comments, I honestly didn't know where to start. Who was this letter to or for? I looked up at Father Priest, still obviously grimacing.

Not the face he'd expected.

I look around the fire and realize everyone else is crying. Not just a little bit either, like hysterically crying. This activity was intended to elicit an emotional response from me. Not just an emotional response, a *hysterical* emotional response.

Oh . . .

For spiritual purposes, obviously.

I've heard Karen talk about God exactly however many times she does in this letter.

We never celebrated my birthday, not a single time. It was always "we'll do it next year!" They had huge parties when the other kids turned sixteen and invited the entire family. But that wasn't *my* life.

The only one-on-one time Karen and I ever had was when she was beating me, manipulating me, or gaslighting me into doing some horrible thing. In fact, the thing she is referencing in "honesty is the best policy" is that, around that time, Marie's daughter, Jessica, and I were in winter guard, overtired together. She accidentally let it slip that I was in foster care and I accidentally called her "a b———h" about it.

We were kids. It was *not* a thing. I also didn't want to snitch on her.

But it got around that we were fighting (we weren't), and this was when Karen made that little thing her excuse to punish Marie. And then Jessica and I weren't allowed to be friends for a little while.

Karen never brought us on vacation when she didn't have to; she almost exclusively left us behind with a babysitter, often total randoms, one of whom actually reported her to DCFS.

We did have a really big Christmas *one year*, though, and she took photos of everything they had purchased for me to gaslight people who would ask. And then she returned them all.

She said she returned all the gifts due to my behavior, but that became a pattern with her.

And here was this letter:

"I bet you didn't think I saw through you like that . . ."

Yes, I did think you saw through me. I *literally* thought that. Narcissists are all practiced manipulators. I was seven, but congratulations?

"I have always kept this secret in my heart, waiting for the right time to tell you: I love you!" And I guess this was the right time? In front of people you wanted me to cry for? A solid ten years too late? Nice. Better late than never.

She'd clearly numbered the note early and tried to fill the pages while having no warm feelings about me. *"Here's a random story? Time to be moving on now . . . ? I'm getting tired of writing . . . ?"*

I could go on and on with this nonsense because clearly she didn't even know what someone would say to someone they actually loved. It is fully outside her experience.

Who knows what she was hoping I'd get out of this letter, if anything. But what I *really* got from this fake letter was that I would never be her daughter to her. There was no "earning it" and that was always what was going to happen, no matter what she said. No matter what she did.

But *I am* grateful for her letter. Because she was right: *Honesty is the best policy.*

So let me be honest: This is an example of what gaslighting looks like with narcissists. This is why you almost never realize they don't *really* love you. This is the letter Karen wrote for her Church while trying to beat the personhood out of me. She was trying to make me what she wanted. With her "molding" and "shaping" and "guidance." But listen: An abuser will always find a reason to hurt you. It just makes them feel good. It has nothing to do with you. It has nothing to do with you "earning" their love. If they're using God as an excuse, that's not God. They will always find people who will enable them in your abuse, and that isn't about you either.

They will always find an excuse.

The Last Day

When I was twenty-one years old, I "aged out" of foster care. Karen had told me and everyone else in the family she had adopted Ted and me when we were younger. That wasn't true. In fact, I should have known something was amiss when I had to go to the courthouse on my eighteenth birthday to legally change my name to their last name because that's what Karen told me to do, "if I wanted to prove I wanted to be in their family."

At the time I aged out, I was dating Todd, who was at college at Emory University in Atlanta. I had just come back from visiting him and some of the smartest kids I knew. These kids were supportive of me and had started calling my foster mother "The Karen" like the monster she was whenever I would talk about my childhood. Todd hated when I talked about myself, but the other kids were cool about it. When you aren't in an abusive situation and your survival isn't at risk day-to-day, a big side effect of that is you can often see the situation from the outside with a little more clarity. That's what was happening to me.

The day I returned from Atlanta, Karen got into a very physical fight with her youngest daughter, Chavonne. By that time, I was *very over* my fear of Karen, so I stepped into her and told her to stop. Karen was incensed at my audacity, and the situation escalated.

I did what a normal grown person would do in a domestic situation that turned violent and told her if she didn't stop, I would call the police.

She started screaming obscenities, so I picked up the phone, and she physically fought it away from me. I left the room to get another phone, and she took them all off the hook so I couldn't dial out.

Calling the police is *the* cardinal sin to abusers who like to operate in the dark, like this woman.

Things escalated from there.

She physically threw me out the door and locked it behind me. I went around to the back door, and everyone had gotten the memo. Becky and Ted stared out at me and laughed, waving. I was locked out and not getting back in. Kids take part in the abuse in these types of families for praise, preferential treatment, or any number of their own drives and desires. Especially older kids.

Undeterred, I walked to the nearest business and asked to use their phone. I called one of my best friends, Chris, who picked me up and brought me to his house to stay with his family, which was incredibly lucky and I will always be grateful to them.

I called home to work out a resolution to the situation but was told I was no longer welcome there.

I had lived with that family since I was seven, and I was abused every day, all under the guise that "at least I was a member of their family and couldn't be cast out into the world alone."

I was *very* wrong.

I called Karen later that night when I happened to see her picking up Ted at the grocery store where he was working at the time. It's a small town. I was sitting in the car with Todd, whose parents sent us to pick up something for them, and saw her pull up. She answered.

"Hi, I was wondering if I could come by and pick up some stuff?" I asked.

"Well, that's not going to work for me," she said.

"Why not?" I asked. "We can go right now."

"Well, I'm out to dinner with Marie,"[52] she said.

"No, you aren't," I said.

I was standing in the actual parking lot looking right at her. She was watching for Ted, facing the door he would come out.

"Don't tell me where I am!" she screamed. "I'm not one of your little friends!"

"No, I mean, you're not out to dinner with Marie. Look to your left. That's me waving at you," I said, now waving like an idiot.

She looked over, made a strangled noise, like some sort of shriek, hung up the phone, and burned rubber getting out of there.

Todd, who came from a more normal, upper-middle-class family, laughed for probably forty-five minutes. I just sat there stunned.

"You saw her, right?" I whispered.

He lit a cigarette.

"Yeah. I saw her. We all see her," he said, finally wiping his eyes from the laughter.

The next day, Karen called my friend Chris on *his* cell to tell him he "may" bring me the next day to pick up my things while she "has witnesses."

Witnesses are a big thing for narcissists. They're always in the middle of some huge novella at the hands of someone who is trying to destroy them.

They accuse you of the very thing *they're doing*.

Chris and I drove over. She handed me a plastic bag with some underwear in it. In front of *said witness*, I begged to take my teddy bear with me and at least some clothes. She agreed that I could take whatever I'd paid for, and ultimately I left with a tiny white laundry basket with my teddy bear and a few other things I could grab.

As I carried out the possessions, I turned to basically the only mother I'd ever known. She was smiling broadly at her friend-witness.

"I'm leaving now. Don't you maybe have anything you want to say to me after all this time?" I asked.

---

52 See how she wanted me to think she was out with the daughter I *already knew* she couldn't stand? Like it would hurt me? Maybe it would hurt her. I like Marie.

Her smug smile turned into a look of surprise, then of false piety, and she said: "Well, I love you, of course!"

I assume the look on my face denoted the horror I was feeling because the smug smile was back.

"Bye!" she said cheerily, waving.

Chris chain-smoked the whole way back to his house.

"I literally can't believe that just happened that way, Di," he finally said.

"Why not?" I asked. "Has anything she has ever done led you to believe she was anything other than the monster she just was? You knew. I've told you."

"Yeah, but not like that," he said, breathing out the smoke. "Not like that."

Incidentally, the lifelong friend-witness she had over was the mother of HomeOwner who hosted the Fourth of July party. *Same family.* Just to give you an idea of what kind of person might be down for the experience of watching something like this happen to a foster kid. Why her? Why would she want to see me thrown out of Karen's house? *Because the secret I was keeping was a threat to her family.* Wild, right? Karen was giving her a "loyalty gift."

I assumed staying with Chris and his family would be over in a matter of days. I thought people in the family would ask where I was, certainly. You can't just make someone disappear and then never hear from them again. I'd lived with the Smiths for more than a decade! They were distant cousins of some of the most established families in town. It was a small town. *People knew me.*

Sure enough, I got a phone call later that month. Karen's eldest daughter, Marie, started in right away when I answered:

"Di?! What the h—l is going on?!"

"Um, well, Ma kicked me out," I said ashamedly.

"What did you do?!" she asked me, alarmed.

I told her what had happened.

"That's not what *she* said," she retorted.

"What do you mean?" I asked. "*What else* could she have said?"

"She said she kicked you out because you called DCFS on Dad [her dad, Willy] and said he had been sexually abusing Chavonne. She had to undergo physical testing[53] to prove he hadn't done that, and it was so traumatic for her that she couldn't have you around anymore, and Ma is just trying to protect Chavonne from someone totally damaged by foster care."

I was floored. So this is why, in a family of ten immediate members (and many more extended ones), nobody took my calls or wondered where I was. She'd thought of everything.

I started to cry. I could never go back. She had won. She'd taken everything. I was alone in the world.

She specifically removed me from any biological family I'd had. She tried to remove me from any friends I had. She tried to keep me from being successful in any way she could just so she could discard me like trash when she wanted.

And when I became a threat who would call the police and expose her, I was no longer worth the trouble it took to control me.

That was in July 2005, and I've never gone back *to this day.*

I later found out that the reason she needed me to change my name when I was eighteen rather than it being done automatically when we were "adopted."

It turns out, *we weren't adopted.* We were put under guardianship. The entire time she was having me work one to two jobs to pay her for "room and board," she was being paid by the State of Massachusetts for the same thing.

That's why I had to undergo so much testing. She had to prove I was worth *more money.* And my birth father, Eddie, was reimbursing the state through wage garnishment. In a strange coincidence, Karen stopped getting paid for me two months before she kicked me out for good.

My younger brother, Ted, had the same suspicious timing when she kicked him out at twenty-one. She had him living homeless behind a shopping center Willy cleaned, sleeping in some of the trucks Willy kept there for work. In the parking lot.

As an adult, I can tell you now that she actually hadn't thought of everything back then. *People just didn't check.* When something like that gets

---

53   Wouldn't Chavonne at least know that couldn't be the truth? Yeah, you'd think.

reported to DCFS, an investigation gets opened and they keep records of all that. That's right.

I called them to ask about my case and, in the least surprising turn of events, no such investigation was ever opened because no such report has ever been made. You can call yourself.

Why didn't she just call and report anonymously and blame it on me so the story she told Marie could be "corroborated"? Because she couldn't take the chance *they'd actually investigate her.*

Karen had made quite a habit of telling stories like this to explain away why members of the family who left were no longer to be spoken of or to. She'd claim they had made false reports to DCFS to try to get us all "put into foster care and raped."

She said her eldest son Keith's first wife did that; she did. She claimed Willy's baby mama had done the same; she hadn't. And she also claimed her eldest son's second wife, Mae, had called DCFS on her way out the door too. She had not. Neither had I.

Her foster home was officially closed by the State when we were all grown.

As kids, it doesn't occur to you that this just isn't normal. Or indeed not as adults around her. She just said these things to control variables once someone left the family and keep us compliant. She also needed to keep us from contacting former family members who had all been kind to us.

Almost all stories that involve her and DCFS are complete and total fabrications. If you're in the family and you're reading this, you don't have to believe me. You can call them yourself; you know the names and dates. It's *all* lies. She's a manipulative, despicable liar who made up the sickest story she could think of for attention and so she could throw away her foster kid without any social consequences.

That was fifteen years ago and most of the immediate family never contacted me. Not to check in. Not to see whether I was doing okay. Not even just to make sure I was alive.

I was dead to the people who had been my family since I was seven. None of them came looking for me except Marie and her kids, who knew the level to which Karen would sink because of Marie's own abuse. They stayed good to me. All of them.

I'd taken care of most of the kids in that house in one way or another. I was there for holidays, school breaks, hockey games, softball games.

We survived that household together.

I did most everyone's homework at one time or another. I drove with the eldest son thirty minutes each way several times a week to pick up and drop off his kids on his visitation days. I helped the second eldest move out from his baby mama's house on one of their break-up tears, when she could have literally killed me. Neil used me as one of the only confidants in the family for all he was going through. I protected Ted from abuse from the time he was born until he turned into a full-blown adult.

Yeah, even Ted doesn't talk to me anymore unless he needs money. He called once for $300 to take his baby mama to the State Fair. I always send money. And Chavonne, who had been calling me crying every night while I was visiting Atlanta because Karen was so awful to her? I never heard from her again. I got thrown out that day for protecting her, and suddenly I didn't exist for her either.

I thought surely by now some of them would have grown up and realized that certainly I mattered. Nope. I went from living in a family with seven other (foster) siblings and two parents to being totally alone in the world. Because Karen said so.

Chavonne "accidentally" reached out to me via Facebook a few years later. I got a friend request when that was a thing and I messaged her back. I told her I loved and missed her but that I was doing better away from Karen and didn't want to risk bringing Karen's poison back into my life if this wasn't *real* outreach. If this was a way for Karen to hurt me, I'd have to delete her friend request. Clearly it was what I thought it was.

I know because of the response. See if you can spot it too:

"Di, the friend request was in error. No one wants to talk to you. I will be doing the deleting."

You know who uses the expression "in error" to describe a mistake? Not a Gen Z teenager.

You know who takes power back in a situation they're embarrassed at by saying "I will be doing the deleting" after I'd threatened to delete her request? Yeah. Me too.

You don't really need to be a genius to hurt people. But you do have to be smarter than I am to hurt me *now*. Sorry, not sorry.

Karen had thrown me to the wolves and couldn't even leave me alone to die. She was still so worried about what I might do she was keeping tabs on me.

Because I didn't die. I was embraced by other black sheep who had also been thrown to the wolves.

And now I'm a writer.

And sharing the truth.

Nana Santos

When I was a child, my grandmother took me to stay at her elder apartments as often as she could. They were rent-controlled and had serious rules about overnight guests, and they especially prohibited taking in your grandchildren.

She recounted to me vividly how heartbroken she had been when DCFS once removed me. My biological aunt remembers that story the best of all of us but, basically, DCFS tore me from Nana Santos's arms and I went screaming into the police car.

But she told me her phone number for emergencies. Over and over again. She made me memorize it.

My grandmother truly loved me. She would hide Hershey's Kisses for me to find in a frog tchotchke she kept in a reachable place. I would sneak over and find the chocolate and, by the time I went back, she had sneaked a new one in. It was a game we played. Or she was magic. Probably both. I still keep Hershey's Kisses on my ofrenda[54] for her absolutely always, and my kids regularly steal them. And, even though I know that's not really allowed, I can hear her laughing about it. I put out too many now and think of the ones they steal as Nana sharing with them. I can't explain that, but I'm sure of it.

---

54 Ancestor offering and remembrance table.

My nana was magic. Don't start with me; I know everyone's nana is magic, but mine *was* for real. She knew things she couldn't know and always knew when it was me calling before there was caller ID. As a result, I'm fully one of those people who believe she was psychic. Yep. It just is. I'm not going to fight.

When I was a kid, Nana told me I was going to have a "magic" that made people tell me about things that were hurting them. As a child, I didn't understand that but, as an adult, people just tell me stuff. *I know.* When I told my partner about this for the first time, I think they thought whatever you must be thinking, but strangers are just immediately comfortable with me.

They come up to me in line at stores, at the beach, everywhere. People see me as somewhere safe to be themselves. They just infodump about whatever is hurting. My partner couldn't deny it anymore once they had witnessed strangers unburdening themselves about a car accident or suicide they'd witnessed seconds into a total-stranger relationship. And I, just as naturally, was prepared to support them with a kind word emotionally like that was the most natural thing in the world.

*Because **it is** for me.*

People just do that. I'm still finding my way through what that means, but I am very used to it. I wish I knew more. But whatever Nana had intended to pass down to me was specifically kept from me by Karen.

I didn't get an opportunity to see Nana again after we were separated from her. Karen pretended to everyone that my biological family were Brown heathens and painted us all with a casual racism brush people accepted just as casually. But, really, she was just a narcissist who needed to make sure I didn't have any loving adults around me who weren't under her control.

Karen used to tell me Nana had called during the day while I was at school because she didn't want to talk to me and because she wanted me to "move on." But she did want to make sure I was being raised "the right way" and "not like a Machado." Karen *loved* to crow that my nana was displeased with my birth father, Eddie. And she was. That's not untrue. But it wasn't for the racist reasons to which Karen subscribed. It was because he used drugs and hadn't kept us safe. But Karen used Nana's disapproval of Eddie to show that she had my nana's blessing in abusing me.

But she did not have Nana's blessing. In fact, it turned out Nana had been sending checks to Karen to feed us until she became suspicious of Karen and started sending grocery store gift cards instead—on her fixed income. But Karen regularly trumpeted about how she was the only one keeping Ted and me off the streets—because we were *so unlovable.*

On top of that, Karen had me working as soon as I could get a work permit (at fourteen years old) to pay her back for her financial loss feeding, clothing, and housing me. So . . . I paid her weekly. My nana paid her. And the state paid her for the "care" I received as a ward of the state, which my father Eddie reimbursed through wage garnishment—for all of us (even Kyle who knows Eddie isn't his father).

Nana started developing health problems around the same time Karen kicked me out of her house. I moved to Atlanta and, after taking some time to settle in, called Nana. No one answered, so I sent her a card. I told her I was doing well and would love to see her now that Karen wasn't keeping us apart. I couldn't wait to be back together with her.

I didn't get a response.

Months later, I got a card from Eddie's sister, my aunt, telling me that Nana had passed away.

She wrote how proud Nana had always been of me and how her whole fridge was covered in newspaper clippings of times I made the news. I never learned how she found out when I'd done something newsworthy. (I assume magic.)

She told me Nana loved me fiercely and that the saddest time in Nana's life had been when DCFS removed us from her. Us being torn from her arms was her worst memory in more than eighty years of living. She told me Nana hadn't wanted to bother me with her illness at the end of her life while I was struggling to survive because there was nothing I could have done.

I had never experienced that kind of grief because I had never had any-thing to lose. Once your family is ripped away from you, you are sort of forever destabilized. Madre Wounds, or Mother Wounds, are lifelong healing journeys. It's like a "bad leg" that gets sore around Mother's Day every year.

My grandmother died just before I got a chance to claw back my relationship with her. Before I got a chance to ask her things. Before I got a chance to know who I was. Before I got a chance to thank her.

Because Karen felt convinced her culture was superior to any culture I could have come from.

Nana was buried in the cemetery we used to play in when I went to Catholic preschool. And I have never found the strength to go and visit her grave.

But I miss her, and I know she's proud of me.

Carpetbagger

If you've never been to Atlanta, I'll describe what Atlanta was for me.

The whole place smells like flowers and clay mud—or, in the heat of summer, overripe peaches. I'd wake up before the sun rose to take two buses to work in Marietta, a city about twenty to thirty minutes north. Even the buses smelled clean, kind of like plastic and crayons.

Atlanta has a tremendous amount of human and cultural diversity. It's 49 percent Black[55] and has the third largest LGBTQ+ population per capita in the US. A true melting pot. Largely because of this diversity, Atlanta is the epitome of cool. I don't mean that in my opinion. Diversity drives innovation; only the best ideas rise to the top. Atlanta has some of the best comfort food, the best music, the best style, and tons of celebrities live there. Usher can be seen regularly on his phone picking up his own Starbucks.

Being at the center of cool in your twenties is an amazing experience. It is actually hard to effectively describe and measure the impact a culture like Atlanta's has on your overall personhood.

Atlanta is warm nine to ten months of the year, so it carries that summer breeze feeling year-round. Most restaurants have outdoor dining options. There's a bar in the Lenox mall where the waitstaff wears crop tops and mini-

---

55   United States Census Bureau, "QuickFacts: Atlanta City, Georgia," Census.gov, 2022, https://www.census.gov/quickfacts/atlantacitygeorgia.

skirts that's pretty popular, and I've heard men working in finance joke that "you can tell when it's spring because of their outfits." Really, in the spring, you can roll down your windows and listen to Ray Charles lamenting his exile from performing in Georgia in "Georgia on My Mind" while flower petals fall from the dogwoods and float in the warm air like a summer snow.

When it rains, the clouds aren't gray and blue like in most places. In Atlanta, they're gray and purple. The storms shake the windows, and the air smells like electricity. Most of the year, the rain is warm.

But what I remember the most is how selflessly kind *most* folks were to me.

My job in Marietta was hard to get to by public transportation, and the owner, Bob, felt bad that I was working so hard to get back and forth to work. I had to take two buses before dawn to get there by 9 a.m. every day, and you definitely didn't want to be in Atlanta's afternoon traffic on I-75 to I-85 highways. There's no rush hour.

Bob was surprised I hadn't quit to get a job closer to my house. I told him I'd made a commitment to him. He knew my story, appreciated my work ethic, and felt like someone could cut me a break every now and then, so he bought a car that he let me use until I could pay him back through my commissions. I needed my base wages for rent, so he let me use just the commissions I earned for selling extra stuff for his business to pay for the car. Apparently, he did this often for folks who worked for him. He never bought them cars but fronted them money when things weren't going their way. He and his family took me under their wings and taught me how to be a person. They all treated each other, me, and other people with kindness and respect. True Christians.

In 2007, Bob and his family found out I didn't have anywhere to go for Thanksgiving after I offered to work that day for the second year in a row.

"What's Todd doing?" Bob asked gently.

"He's going home to be with his family," I answered.

"Why aren't you going with him?"

"Because his parents don't like me, and he doesn't like reminding them I live here. It apparently causes arguments."

"Why doesn't he stick up for you?"

"Well, you know, they're fancy and I grew up in foster care."

"That's not a thing. If he loved you, he'd want to spend the holidays with you."

I shrugged.

"Well, if you don't have anything going on, Miss Jan and I would love to have you and your pups over for Thanksgiving."

I tried to graciously turn him down, but he wouldn't hear of it. He told me to meet him at the office at lunchtime and had me follow him to his beautiful house.

No one else was there. It was just Bob and Miss Jan. They had purchased food from Boston Market and created a holiday table just for me—just so *I* had somewhere to go. Who was I to them? No one.

I was their employee. Just some girl who didn't come from anywhere. But that wasn't how they felt. They felt like I was a good person who didn't deserve the hand I was dealt and was just trying to make the most of it.

They supported me from that day on. Like family. Their son John still texts me to offer business insights and ideas or to check on my kids. John straight up retired in his forties and his daughters are gorgeous geniuses; you want John's advice on things.

I visited Atlanta before the pandemic, and they made time to see me even though they hadn't been feeling well. I'll visit again this year and plan to go back every two years in perpetuity. When my partner wanted to ask me to marry him, he called Bob to ask his permission, which he got. Bob took that responsibility seriously and grilled him like crazy. I am still moved by that.

If I hadn't moved to Atlanta, I would never have learned how important it was to create your own family, or how to do it. Maybe you were born into hellacious garbage like I was. Maybe you were moved in and out of terrible foster homes after that. Maybe you were homeless and living on a friend's couch in his parents' basement. You still are worthy of family, and yours is out there waiting for you to find them, just like mine was in Bob and Miss Jan.

Their family is Southern Republican, and it was *such a thing* that I wasn't. They announced it like I had some weird disease that they were going to all love and tolerate about me.

"Di is a liberal, but we love her anyway, and we're gonna pray for her," they announced when I started working for them.

I'm sure they're still praying for me. I'm still a liberal, I guess, by American standards. But they love me anyway even though they are definitely still conservative; they always were. If my ideas are worth anything, they can stand a good fight. If my love is worth anything, it'll bridge our differences when it can.

Atlanta was exactly the place I needed to be to change everything about where I was going and turn me into who I was going to be. It's a kinder, gentler city. Somewhere where I could afford to stay alive and thrive. I owe my success in large part to Atlanta and the people I met there. It's my hometown.

I made it because Atlanta wanted me to.

The Framers

One summer, I interned for the DeKalb County Child Advocacy Center in Atlanta. I was the only non-law student intern in the program. They put us all through several days of training at Emory University, so it was not cheap, and I appreciated the opportunity. I still love everyone there. I only got "in trouble" there one time, and it was because I *accidentally* told a Black woman to "relax." Literally my fault. Let me explain.

I was organizing the tiny desk they set aside for me. All the other interns had actual desks they shared with each other. I was trying to look busy and pretended I had more stuff to organize, like they were. They had law books, computers, and pictures of their families.

Suddenly, the head paralegal was standing over my cube. This is how our conversation went:

Debbie: "I regret to inform you that all the *other* interns took up all the waste baskets. There are no more. There is no way they will ever ask for money for baskets for interns. You'll have to share."

Me: "Oh, no worries. You can totally relax, I don't mind."

She spun on her heel and left without saying anything, but I knew I had done something wrong. I thought maybe I hadn't received her words with enough hand-wringing but wasn't sure.

Seriously, fancy people are a completely different frame of reference for me. With my ADHD, I used to always be guessing at human behavior because people's mouths say one thing but their body language says the opposite, and my brain processes both. Then, a third thread pops in and I wonder, *Why the lie?* And then another, *Ah! you aren't paying attention!* And, finally, another thread will process what is happening *in the context of where we are.* Are these fancy people? How fancy? It matters. The context of why we're lying to each other matters, otherwise my brain will seek the answers out while I should be listening. Usually it's out of politeness. It's about following the rules about how we talk to each other in the context of our relationships, identities, and priorities. There's also next-level context in non-white relationships.

For example, if I am speaking Spanish with another Spanish speaker and a non-Spanish speaker enters, do we switch to English for their benefit? Sometimes. It depends on the context of our relationship with that person and our safety at continuing in Spanish. Are they safe to be speaking Spanish in front of? If that person tries to enter the conversation and we know they only speak English, we usually switch to English. It would be rude not to. You switch to the shared language. Unless he's the creepy guy at work and in that case "no hablo inglés."

Context. It informs all of our conversations, and neurodiverse people like me process it all separately, simultaneously, and often consciously.

I was listening to Debbie. But I was also high anxiety, and trauma leaves me with a stress-gap I have to close silently in normal interactions with people.

I couldn't breathe from the anxiety of what unbelievable sin I could've committed.

Fortunately, she didn't make me wait.

Debbie was suddenly standing beside my basketless desk as if she had appeared there.

Poof, you're fired.

"See me in the supply closet, please," she said.

"Can I follow you there? I don't know where anything is . . ." I started to ask, but she walks fast. Purposeful.

I'm fired on the first day because I didn't belong here.

She held the door for me as we both entered, me following her. Then she spun to face me. There is no spit in my mouth and she can surely hear my heart.

"Look, you offended me today, and I want to get it off my chest . . ." she began.

Fortunately, I had no air in my lungs, so I didn't accidentally interrupt her with ADHD brain in a high-stress situation. Sometimes I immediately minimize.

". . . you told me to 'relax' and I didn't appreciate it," she finished.

My brain panicked. I was in a full *Inside Out*[56] moment.

You did what?!

Fortunately, with her having taken me aside, I wasn't processing all the other info around her and *I stopped digging*.

"Oh my God! I *did not* mean to suggest you should 'relax.' I would never! I was picking up from your energy that you were already angry about dealing with this, and I come from foster care, so I was trying to minimize it by making it a nonissue for you. In case *I* was the reason there weren't any left. It's a trauma response. Also, I have ADHD, which is responsible for this over-share. Please don't fire me. I'll have to keep waitressing forever."[57]

All in a single breath.

She considered me.

"Thank you for saying that. I *was* angry at having to deal with the baskets. You weren't the only one who didn't get one. A lot of those kids out there have never had to share before, and they are real entitled about it . . .

"So *you're* the Foster Kid?" she asked.

"Yes."

You do not want to back talk in these situations. All responses that don't specifically answer the question asked are considered back talk. I've checked. And now I knew she didn't like those other entitled kids.

"I'm sorry they're being awful. Can I help?" That's all I said. Worth it.

---

56 If you haven't seen this amazing Pixar movie, it follows the journey of emotions coming online as a human. I cried the whole way through. Millennials are all in a toxic relationship with Pixar now. I can admit it.

57 Waitressing is amazing, and I love people. But it doesn't quite fill my spirit.

She and I were cool the rest of the summer and, once I was cool with the head paralegal, I was cool with all of them. And they ran *everything*, even—especially—the attorneys, which gave me some space to be a little less weird and a little more specific-genius space. I got to do a lot of really impactful work in a really short amount of time there. I helped develop the transitioning youth curriculum trying to help kids transition from foster care to adulthood.

I was surprised I had anything to add there, but the child advocate lawyers there really cared about their clients, so they asked really specific questions:

"Di, I have a client who won't go get her driver's license. She needs it to work, but she won't go. Any guesses?" one asked, for example.

After considering it for a moment, I told her, "It's because they might say 'no.' For example, I don't have my passport yet because I'm scared they'll say 'no.'"

Not seeing recognition on her face, I continued: "See, in foster care, a lot of the time your paperwork gets messed up. Your records get lost or messed up. Your name is weird. You have your birth name, maybe, and the one you use. And we've all been in situations, usually at school first, in which we are rejected from something we really want—or need—because there's no central adult or adults keeping track of us. So we're too scared to try and be rejected."

She considered what I said.

"Can you write down your phone number? I'm going to need to call you in the future," she said and then pointed to her door and said, "Leave my door open, please."

I handed her my number and started for the door, but she stopped me. While picking up her phone and dialing out, she said:

"Di?"

"Yes, ma'am?" I responded, spinning around.

"You have until the end of the year to apply for your passport. I'm going to check. Am I understood?" she asked, holding up the paper with my number on it.

I started to answer, but she was already on the call. Fighting for justice everywhere.

Okay. Definitely. I can do that.

I now have my passport, in case you're wondering. She was right.

Tips

In college, I worked at an all-night diner across the way from the Pink Pony, one of Atlanta's most famous strip clubs. It's not their most notorious strip club; that's the Clermont Lounge, and we all know it. I would never write it, but being waitstaff for Atlanta's nightlife in those days could have been its own book. I was there in the days when Jermaine Dupri was writing about "Welcome to Atlanta."

There's a power balance at play in the US service industry, whether we acknowledge it or not. People are paid largely in tips. People they serve get to decide how much money they deserve for the job they did waiting on them. Customarily in the US, people tip 20 percent of the bill, but a lot of people are of the mindset that the 20 percent is "yours to lose," and it gives them a power trip. You have to be nice to them no matter what. You have to tell them they're right. You have to agree and bow or you won't get paid. And then you don't eat. Because of that, service workers often have to smile through absolutely inhumane treatment.

An inordinate number of people come to mid-tier restaurants for exactly that purpose.

Like with any service job, I wasn't given the diner's best shifts when I first started (I worked weekend overnights). I'd start my shift by cleaning up from the night before and end my shift by waiting on folks coming from church on Sunday mornings.

The first breakfast diners would be the dancers coming in from the night before, still winding down. Next were older folks and folks who came in every morning for breakfast regardless of the day. They often overlapped with the dancers leaving. People with kids overlapped with those folks leaving and then churchgoers came in after church, except for Baptists who *were* coming from church and yet it was midday. Bless them. Everything about the Southern Baptists was a blessing, by the way. If you go to a Baptist church in Atlanta even once in your life, nothing else will seem like "church" again. It is a spiritual experience.

One such churchgoing morning, I was waiting on a table of four. The elder sat to my right with three other grown well-dressed people whose relationships with the elder were unknown to me. He was geared up as I tried to rattle out my usual greeting, ordering for everyone, to their dismay. As I looked around the table, no one met my eye.

I recognized this behavior. They didn't want to get invested in me *personally* because they knew this man was going to bully me, and it would be worse for them if they did. I knew this behavior because I knew this kind of guy. He is someone who has to dominate me in front of the people he is with, potentially even in an unsafe way for me.

I read the gentleman back his exact order. He ordered an omelet for himself and recited to me the ingredients he wanted. He did the same for everyone else's orders, which were different kinds of pancakes. All fine.

When their order came, I rushed it right out to them. I did not want to give this guy any reason to lash out in public, especially not in my direction. No offense, World. But no such luck.

I sat nearby, hoping to not unleash his inevitable wrath on any of my coworkers. That's not how you make friends. I say inevitable because this kind of person enjoys lashing out at people who have no power to actually hold them accountable for their tantrums.

An abuser will always find an excuse.

He looked up, searching the diner for me. As soon as he saw me, he loudly snapped his fingers above his head in my direction. I *love* when they snap at you.

I approached him cautiously.

"Is everything all right with your breakfast, sir?" I asked.

"No! Everything is NOT all right! My omelet doesn't have any cheese in it!" he fumed.

I got out my notepad.

"I'm sorry, sir. You didn't list cheese in your ingredients when you told them to me or when I read them back to you. I didn't know you wanted cheese in your omelet."

He was incredulous.

"WHO ON EARTH doesn't want cheese in their omelet?!"

"Sir, I apologize. I thought perhaps you didn't eat cheese. You don't seem like you unintentionally leave things out in your instructions. I didn't guess. I can have it fixed right away."

I had won over his party and some of the people clearly listening to my misery nearby, as people do in close diner quarters. He noticed this too. This was behavior with which I was very familiar in public spaces. A narcissist waiting for an audience so they could win over everyone listening. He tried again, loudly and confidently declaring, "Young lady, 'omelet' means 'cheese' in French!"

Everyone listening in immediately had exactly the same thought at once: *It absolutely does not.*

I tried again. "Sir, I can have the kitchen redo it for you immediately."

But this man doubled-down.

"'Omelet' means 'cheese' in French!" He yelled it a little louder so people might agree.

They didn't.

I leaned in.

"Sir," I whispered. "It absolutely *does not* mean 'cheese' in French. *Please.* Can I fix it for you?"

He looked around at the people sitting near him who were clearly more horrified by the mistake than the behavior.

"No, no, thank you, ma'am. This will be perfectly fine," he said.

"Thank you, sir," I said. "Enjoy your breakfast."

On the tip line, he wrote, "the customer is always right." And left no additional money for that little misadventure.

The customer is always right at a mid-tier dining experience. Yes. Except when they are just *objectively wrong*.

Another time a group of musicians came in at midday demanding to be seated in the back section of the diner, which was closed off because I was the only server working. I let them sit in the back corner booth, which had been darkened by my manager. They were fully high when they arrived. So I gave my usual spiel.

The one to my left asked, "What's good here?"

"Well, sir, it's a diner. Everything here is diner food. It's all pretty good," I said.

"Yeah, but like, what's your favorite thing?" he asked.

"I get the grilled cheese a lot," I said.

"Right, but like, say we was out to dinner and this was the menu . . ."

Say I'd accepted you on a date because I'm just a lowly diner waitress, so my consent is obviously taken for granted? Cool. I decided to play even dumber, because, hey, it's $2.50 an hour, and you get what you pay for. Plus I had all day.

"I can afford everything on this menu and I still get the grilled cheese for lunch. So probably I'd get the grilled cheese," I said. "I don't eat meat."

Then I swear to God, this man leaned as far back as he could, took off his shades, scrunched[58] up his face, appraised my body, and said, "Girl, you lyin', you definitely eat meat."

His friends were roaring laughing.

They ordered three full steak dinners, overcooked, fries, no potatoes, and subbed salads for vegetables. All in, that's probably $60, or more, in food. They left, and on the tip line he left me his number. Which, no.

Another time there was a customer who went to Emory University, the nearest college, who decided he was in love with the idea of me. When he

---

58 If you know, you know.

asked the elderly diner owner for my number, she gave him the number to the diner. He called every single day to chat with me while I was at work and I had to brush him off daily. Ironically, it got *me* in a ton of trouble with *her* because "my friends were always calling."

She had given him the number.

When I finally had to tell this guy off, he flew into a rage.

"How dare you?! Do you know who my father is?" he fumed. "YOU'RE A DINER WAITRESS!"

"Right, but like, you called me," I said.

"You aren't even *that* hot! You would be a waste of anyone's time or energy! You should be glad I'm calling! You should be grateful!" he fumed.

"Right, okay, dude, I'm at my place of work. It sounds like you're the class of person who should know: Service people aren't your friends. We *have* to be nice to you. *We're at work.* I am working my way through college at a diner. I didn't ask for your interest. I'm out in public because I have to work, not because I'm looking for your attention. I AM AT WORK!"

He paused for a moment and considered his next plan of attack. He certainly wasn't considering what I'd said.

"Right, but like I just don't understand why you gave me your phone number if you aren't interested," he said.

"Which number??" I said, trying to recall a time I'd ever given my number to a customer, which was never.

"THIS NUMBER, you stupid b——h!"

"THE *DINER NUMBER*?!" I shrieked, incredulous.

At this point, my also fully-Hispanic kitchen staff had rolled up, hearing my alarm.

The taller one gave me the international non-white person nod, which is a quick head tilt up that comes from the chin and means, "What's up, ma?"

I covered the mouthpiece and quickly relayed in Spanish what had taken place. Joy shone on this man's face briefly, and he relayed to his friend in a slightly different kind of Spanish than he and I spoke about what had transpired. His friend also smiled broadly and gave "the nod."

He turned his attention back to me and said in English, "He is speaking Spanish?"

I shook my head.

"Gringito," he said to his friend, as he held out his hand to take the phone from me.

Now, culturally, I don't really have a choice here in him taking this situation over. My Irish side might, but *we weren't all Irish*. I handed him the phone.

He spoke softly but clearly, but the caller was still yelling.

"Oyé! Mira! You call or you bother Diana again, we['re] gonna come to you[r] house and we gonna kill you."

Then he pressed the button to end the call, adjusted his clothing, and made a motion cutting across his throat with his thumb to his friend and me. Well, that's over. They both nodded at each other at a job well done. Then he asked me whether I wanted some food. And yes, obviously I did.

But that guy never called or came by again, and I never got in trouble for how it was dealt with.

I was surprised.

Because apparently his dad was a really big deal.

The diner being so central to interstate 85 and a four-star hotel brought in some amazing meetups too. There was regularly a fetishes meetup where a group of people came to the diner dressed up in their fetish-wear for lunch and to play board games.

One person was in a motorized wheelchair in full Strawberry Shortcake attire. And when I ran to hold the swinging doors for her, she read me the riot act about helping her without her having asked.

"I'm so sorry," I said. "These doors open out and I wasn't sure you could hold them both open and pass through in a wheelchair at the same time. I wasn't even thinking of your feelings."

She considered me to see whether I was being sarcastic. I wasn't. I was just worried.

"Fine," she said. "You can hold the door and I will go through it. But *don't touch* my chair without my consent *at all* because it is part of my body."

"I would never!" I said, aghast.

She chortled.

"What's your name?"

"Di," I said. "Like the princess."

"Well, Di-like-the-princess, what's your kink?"

Strawberry was trying to shock me. That's how she regained power in these situations, I thought. Pushing the other person outside of their comfort zone. But little did Strawberry know, that's where I live. I kept my face expressionless and leaned in.

"It's people who read books and aren't rude to waitstaff," I said.

Strawberry roared with laughter.

"Di-like-the-princess, will you escort me to the table? I'd like to introduce you to the other dolls."

And after that, Strawberry and I were friendly. She just didn't like the idea of people assuming she couldn't do something because of her chair. And as an ADHD-er, I didn't like the idea of someone sitting outside feeling ashamed, left out, or too embarrassed to ask for help just because the stupid door wasn't accessible. That's just bad design.

She and I got more friendly over her visits. We had long arguments about humans. I argued that most people suffer from the bystander effect in situations they haven't encountered before.

I think if you haven't been in the situation before, it's easy to say you'd help or that you'd know what to do. But in my experience, most people avoid the potential for conflict.

Strawberry argued that a lot of people who *do* help people do so for their own selfish reasons, and she doesn't want to be part of that. Strawberry said, "If people were getting off on [her], [she] should be consenting." As a foster kid, I certainly get that. We agreed that I would quietly ask someone if they need help before I just help. But I am allowed to help if someone says they need it.

Now you know too.

The night shift was 8 p.m. to 8 a.m. Friday, Saturday, and Sunday. Then I'd have school all week. I made rent just working weekends. It was a great time. But when I joined the night shift, I realized the vibe in the diner, much like the city itself, changes by time of day—*dramatically*. A lot of super wild stuff happened.

One time a famous, blond Barbie doll-looking exotic dancer sat down in my booth with her Yorkie and some guy. Barbie was adamant she couldn't drink the water because the variation from place to place in the US gave her headaches. As she sat there lovingly feeding her Yorkie, the guy got up to go to the bathroom.

While he was in the bathroom, I chatted up this super gorgeous woman and politely inquired as to her relationship status with her companion. Her stripper shoes[59] had hearts on them and I like dogs.

"Who? Oh, him?" she said, indicating the area he'd walked off to. "He's my assistant! He carries my stuff and my dog so I don't. I pay for everything!" she enunciated the last part to punctuate her point. "Aren't you sweet?" she said, dismissing me.

That's a thing in Atlanta. People dismiss you with things that sound like compliments. And that's a thing for women who date women. If you try to hit on them at all, it just sounds like friendly compliments.

I don't know how to flirt. I think *"Don't sound gay"* to myself and then come back with "Girl, those shoes are divine!" It's fine, I'm married now.

When I went back to the wait station, Barbie's companion, but not her Ken, strolled up behind me and slowly pulled out his wallet. He was wearing jeans that went over his leather loafers, with a navy blue polo tucked in, and a fully open neck to expose his graying chest hair.

Okay, guy.

"She didn't try to pay, did she?" he asked.

"I'm sorry?" I asked, in return.

"My girlfriend," he said, indicating where Barbie was sitting. "She didn't try to pay, did she?"

He handed me his card.

"Um, nope, she didn't," I said.

None of my freaking business.

---

59 She said she was a famous traveling exotic dancer. I wasn't assuming.

"Good," he said. "I'm tired of this feminist BS these days! Glenn Beck is right! Feminists are ruining the country!" he whispered to me.

Impotent rage. Nice.

"Hey, you want to hear a joke?" he asked.

"No, thank you, I don't like jokes," I lied.

"Yes, you do, everybody likes jokes!"

Perfect.

"What is the best way to prevent unwanted teenage pregnancy?" He didn't wait, but I knew he wouldn't. "Bayer brand baby aspirin! She holds it between her knees and then she won't get pregnant!" he said, laughing at his own joke.

This is a weird way to bleed out whatever inequity he felt at their nonrelationship. By coming to the diner to assert dominance over the nearest young woman without the power to hold him accountable for it.

I see why she isn't dating you, dude.

I ran the card as she stood up, tired of waiting, shouting out his name. He snatched the card out of my hand, signed the check, and left no tip. Then he sneered in my face and ran out into the night after her.

I guess I should've asked for her number.

Another time, I was waiting on an Alcoholics Anonymous group that went out to dinner instead of drinking. I called them my Pottery Club so they didn't feel weird. When I was checking one guy out, because they all paid separately, he stopped me.

"I feel like I have to tell you something," he said.

Here it comes.

"When I was in the navy, I was bunking with this guy who everyone found out was gay. He committed suicide by hanging himself and I found him. I can't forget. That's why I drink. I drink so I can forget him. I needed to tell you."

I handed him back his card, and he signed his paperwork and left.

That just happens to me.

One of the funniest things people would ask when I told them where I worked was whether any famous rappers went there. Atlanta is loudly home to rappers.

And yes. Many, and that's none of my business.

"Did any of them have black cards?" is always the next question and, no, none of them did. However, I did see one once, from a guy who owned a hotel downtown. How was it different? It was heavier than you'd expect. I didn't think it was going to fit in the machine when I ran it, but it went through fine. Obviously.

One time it was the middle of the night and it had been a Big Night at the Pony. They got closed down early by the police, and the overflow wave of buzzed people crashed directly into us.

A fight broke out almost immediately. Fortunately, I was backed-up by a marine waiting tables, too, plus an entire kitchen staff of Hispanic people happy to help peacocking men with exiting the premises.

Two men took off equally flashy shirts and started pressing their chests together, each daring the other to make the first move.

Square up.

Then the point of no return:

One man poked the other in the chest.

For the life of me, every man-fight I've seen includes this. I call it the "Man Poke."

So these gentlemen are helped out, and we have to comp all that food. Unfortunately, the dancers had also arrived by that point, with even more folks trailing them. But they don't carry on being dancers when they leave the Pony. The boundaries are serious. As we were cleaning up the mess, I noticed my shirt has been ripped by a patron who grabbed *me* in the fight. Before he was bodied by the marine—who was smiling at the time, incidentally.

But I was unable to see that one of the patrons was bothering one of the dancers. I was on my way back out of the bathroom when I heard her say, "Get the f——k away! Can't you see me eating with my friends?"

The guy got real apologetic and sort of bowed and returned to his seat.

I watched the situation out of the corner of my eye, but there was a lot going on and they weren't in my section. So by the time I got back to it, the dancers were on their way out. I got the impression that this creepy guy continued to bother her throughout her meal because she was yelling at him to leave her alone as she was exiting.

The next thing I knew, the dancer was drawing on the glass from outside the building with the can of whipped cream we used for pancakes and waffles. Then, she whipped off her top, pressed her chest into the whipped cream, and cackled a string of expletives (at the guy, I assume). And then she ran off hysterically laughing. With my whipped cream.

People are wild overnight in Atlanta.

Shadow Boxing

I t's hard to be in a relationship with someone who has sustained the type of trauma I have, I would imagine. I was a bad girlfriend until maybe my mid-twenties. On the one hand, I was possessive, and on the other, I was always ready to leave the relationship first. And, like any traumatized adult with ADHD, *I attract narcissists.*[60]

My relationship with Todd started when I was in my early twenties. I was still living with the Smiths but only just. He had been raised differently than anything I had ever experienced. He had been taught he was above people like us. People like the Smiths. In fact, Karen was so taken in by him (another narcissist) and what a relationship with him might lead to, she actually tried to get him to dump me and go out with Becky who was six years younger than me. I'm not kidding. She tried to set my college-aged boyfriend up with her fifteen-year-old adopted daughter. She'd try to convince him how much prettier and "less of a hassle" Becky was. We talked about how weird it was constantly, probably because it stroked his ego. After a while, though, I started not letting him come in when he picked me up. I wasn't mad; I had grown past mad. *I was resigned.* Karen thought I was trash and that he was miles above me.

---

60   Yes. I have been told that narcissists aren't picky and they glom on to everyone and that "it's more like my ADHD doesn't notice their bad behavior." Most folks will just drop them. But it's pretty hard to psychically predict intent in humans. That's why we get so good at people-reading, eventually. Safety.

It was okay. *His* parents felt that way too. Loudly. It was a lot to carry.

Todd's story was that his dad, Mr. Big, grew up on "the wrong side of the tracks too." So I idolized him. I told him so. Whenever I had to be in Mr. Big's presence, I spent the entire time apologizing for my existence. I'm embarrassed to admit that now, as an adult, but I let this man run me around. Mostly I cringe because now I know Mr. Big wasn't from "the wrong side of the tracks"; he was solidly middle class. Mr. Big lived with both parents in a nice town and went to all private schools. He was just *less rich* than his classmates at said private schools and, apparently, they never let him forget it. That chip was learned—and passed down. Another "self-made" man who bragged about being self-made. In my experience, people like me who are wholly self-made aren't *really* going out of our way to remind people about it. You can take that news to the bank.

Around 2006, Todd started feeling like he was above me too. Like all narcissists, he stopped "love-bombing" me and began to pull back. It happened so slowly that I didn't even fight it. It would be one small line crossed after another but never enough so you'd notice. Or fight it.

When Todd was graduating from college, his whole family was coming down to Atlanta to see him. I wasn't allowed to go. I lived there, in Atlanta, where he went to college. They were coming into town, and I was supposed to stay as far away as possible to keep the peace. So I didn't go to see my boyfriend graduate from college. I worked that day. My work friends were beside themselves. Especially Bob, who owned the business.

I didn't go to dinner with Todd and his family either. I wasn't invited. I didn't really see Todd at all that weekend. He asked me to meet him to help him pack after he dropped his family off at their hotel. So I walked two miles to Emory from my apartment to help him move out of the dorms, after 10 p.m. in the dark. But he never came home. Fortunately, someone recognized me from another dorm and let me into the hallway so I didn't have to sit outside or walk two miles back by myself. I sat outside his door until midnight when he stumbled in drunk and passed out. After that, that attitude from him kind of became my new normal. I was entirely alone in the world outside of him, thanks to him isolating me right after I'd been thrown away by Karen. It wasn't great.

His parents came by the next morning and moved Todd's boxes from his dorm to my apartment to keep from having to pay storage fees. I thought, *Well, this is a win. They're acknowledging me.* But they dropped Todd's boxes in my living room and then left without saying a word. The three of them.

They just didn't think I was a person and had no problem showing it. Weirdly, they didn't treat Todd that well either and, somehow, deluded themselves into thinking I was angling for some sort of gold digger spot in their upper-mid-range family. It wasn't like they were living next door to Taylor Swift at Holiday House. *Then, maybe.*

By the way, you know who gatekeeps "class separation"? People who feel they are *just barely* in their desired class. This is true of literally all human groups of status or identity we put ourselves in. Gatekeepers feel insecure about *their* place.

Once, when Todd was a sophomore, he miscalculated his food budget and ran out of money. Mr. Big was so pissed that he wouldn't speak to him about it. Todd called his mother crying and hungry.

I told you, hunger makes you feel pretty scared.

According to Todd, his mom told him, "Borrow some rice from a friend. It costs like $2."

I was disgusted. I knew for a fact neither one of his parents had ever gone hungry, so it was pretty telling that they were so cavalier about it with Todd. I called down to the local Domino's and sent half the menu. Meat Lovers' pie, sides, everything.

I worked for every single cent I had, and I still had more grace in my heart for that kid than they did. These days I would've just done the economical thing and sent money for groceries, but I was still very much a kid then.

Todd got a job working for a big consulting company, The Consulting Company,[61] right out of Emory. The job didn't start until July, so he flew to Boston

---

61   I have to pay my bills, y'all. I don't want trouble with anyone who didn't start a fight with me first.

until the job started. Our friends were pretty shocked that it was going down that way. I wasn't alone though. My friend Jason,[62] for example, would come over and eat chips with me while I watched all my terrible DVDs on my tiny TV. We watched *Con Air* like thirty times, and he was never inappropriate or weird. He just acted like a friend who understood Spanish slang and liked to eat chips.

Another thing that started happening around then with Todd was the clear implication that I was the favorite in our relationship. He'd introduce me to people he worked with at The Consulting Company and they would *all* adore me and they would be kind of medium rare on him.

I asked this guy what he was working on at The Consulting Company, and he said, "Oh, no, I don't want to talk about that. What are *you* doing?"

"I'm not fancy like you guys," I said. "I work in an office."

"Oh please," he said. "We're all sick to death of talking to each other."

"Other people at The Consulting Company?" I asked.

"Well, yeah, them and basically *all* rich people," he said, gesturing around to everyone in the room. He smiled more broadly at me.

I'm interesting. Huh. Imagine my surprise. And probably at least kind of pretty too because, at the time, honestly, I wasn't *that* interesting. No one was in their early twenties. I can admit that.

But Todd knew how they felt.

So, whenever I had to attend an event for The Consulting Company, I just made as many friends as I could. I met some extraordinary people who are doing amazing things now. I was like the sauce that made all these geeks cool to each other. Isn't that fascinating? In the end, they wanted to be around me instead. Because of silly things like ordering dessert and listening to my positions on geekdom "to-the-death" arguments.

This was kind of a turning point for me. I understood I didn't have to be rich to be smart. These smart people who were working diligently to become masters of the universe weren't interested in Todd because Todd had been

---

62   Jason is still an awesome friend. He's doing well at work. He has a nice dog. Some people raise good humans, and his parents did. I feel like they'd want to know. Thanks for sticking by me.

raised in his father Mr. Big's insecurities. Todd thought he was above me and that these people were above him. People at The Consulting Company didn't feel that way, and they thought he was a douche for thinking that of me.

They started not inviting him to things. They started not putting him on their projects. Every time he walked into a situation there, he assumed management would want to see someone "managing and delegating" the tasks they had just delegated to the associates. Like middle management.[63] He just did not get that sometimes to be successful you have to roll up *your own sleeves, not just other people's.* He was "on the beach"[64] often, and he was getting really depressed about it. Most days he'd walk down to the nearest dive bar and just sit on a stool, smoking and drinking all day, while I was at school or work.

I eventually threatened to call his parents if he didn't get help for what turned out to be a pretty significant case of alcoholism. It did no good. He just left the house pretending to go to AA meetings and did whatever . . . probably went back to the bar . . . definitely cheated on me.

In my desperation to get him better, I started inviting his colleagues to our apartment. I could cook pretty well and the senior partners liked me a lot. They'd often tell me if I ever needed a job, they'd be thrilled to have me.

I'd go to their social dinners and convince their wives and partners to get dessert with me, or margaritas when they were supposed to be drinking wine. Or they'd gather around me after hearing "casually from someone" about my upbringing for impromptu social justice talks over jalapeño poppers.

They loved how different I was. Everyone else was fighting to fit in, but I had no option but to be comfortable standing out. People felt warmed by my presence and just poured out all their secrets to me. Smart people. Educated people. If you can judge a person by whom they surround themselves with, I was intentional with my energy.

And I was lucky to be a funny, queer, bartender-esque secret-keeper who was the underdog friend of many a powerful Atlanta wife. Obviously, that

---

63   Remember that exchange at the end of *Ever After* where Anjelica Huston's fabulous
      character Baroness Rodmilla de Ghent gets knocked into the laundry dye? It was like that.
64   Not staffed on a project.

didn't hurt me. But there is no one on earth who could rightly claim I'm here because they enabled it. If I'm anything, I'm a product of my community.

"You should write a book," they'd say.

Suddenly me being who I already was, was exactly what people living in Atlanta wanted to see from me.

It was a game changer. Way less of a pressure to fit into some type of box I was often asked to fit into.

For most of our relationship, Todd told me he couldn't defend me to Mr. Big due to my overall worthlessness—and I stupidly agreed. Basically, they were right; I wasn't in his league, right? Not so much. More and more it was starting to seem as if we weren't equals, but it was because *he* was beneath *me*.

Georgia State

My romantic relationship with Todd was circling the drain when I got into college at Georgia State, another milestone that changed me forever.

I excelled at everything I tried, except for art history, I won't lie. I signed up for art history, but the professor taught building history. Buildings as art. I have ADHD and all those things are buildings. My bad.

The people I was at school with loved me. I had already figured out how to be comfortable being myself and that's really attractive to people finding their own stride in college. I lost thirty pounds, largely due to stress and Todd naming my stomach fat roll "Leon."[65] That made me more confident and made me speak up even more. I stood up when I felt like people were being excluded, and I found my voice as a leader. This wasn't a junior college; this was a big school. We had a football team.

Todd started begging me to go to sporting events at Georgia State and then started regressing back to his college days. He really wasn't doing so great out in real life. That made him even meaner and overeager to be the thirty-year-old at college parties flashing grown money around. He became who his father wanted him to become after college but had

---

65 Like the *Airplane* movie. Yep.

no idea what to do now once he got there. He wasn't happy. And I had become his enemy.

The more successful I became, and the taller I stood, the more Todd tried to cut me down.

For example, I framed all my awards and hung them on the walls in the living room. We'd fight constantly about that. *I did it* because it gave me a little boost to feel like I was finally getting to where I wanted to be. Because of my ADHD, I was worried I'd quit right at the end in my usual pattern of trauma-induced self-sabotage, so my awards motivated me to keep on track. But he'd find ways to hurt me whenever a new one went on the wall. Not physically. He was no match for me, physically, because I grew up with hockey-player brothers in foster care. He was a talker, a gaslighter.

One night when I was just about to graduate from college, I had a ten-page research paper to turn in the next day. He invited me to dinner "to celebrate." We were "off" in our relationship, but he was trying to convince me he'd changed and to take him back. Those of you who know a narcissist may know where this is going, but I was a stupid kid suffering from trauma and wanted to believe him. I wanted to believe we could still be friends.

Anyway, I was wrapping up my conclusion and editing the paper. I only needed two hours max to finish it. His friend Chad had invited him to the Sweetwater Festival[66] in Georgia, and they both agreed he'd be there for a couple of hours. I thanked Chad and wished them both a good time. I finished my paper and emailed it to my professor. I also prepared a couple of thoughts for the upcoming final's essays while they were fresh in my mind. I rushed to shower and get ready for dinner. I was ready by eight and I hate to be rushed.

Todd never came back. Just at all. He didn't answer my calls or my texts. Chad didn't answer my calls or my texts. I waited up until I finally got a call from him at 3 a.m.

"Hey!" he hissed into the phone. He hissed when he was drunk.

You have to be kidding me.

---

66   Sweetwater is a super popular local brewery.

"Are you calling to let me know you're in the hospital?" I asked sarcastically.

"What? No. Shut up. Listen, you need to come pick me up . . ."

"What do you mean, 'I need to come pick you up?' Where's Chad?" I asked.

"He left a long time ago," Todd reported tersely.

"Then where were you?" I asked.

"You need to come get me. There aren't any cabs and Chad left me here with this girl," he shouted audaciously into the phone as the wind whipped past him.

"The what?" I asked, dumbfounded.

"Look, can you come pick me up?"

"Are you freaking kidding me? I'm absolutely not doing that," I said.

He laughed. *Laughed.*

"Whatever, I'm up the street now. See you when I get there," and then he hung up on me.

Minutes later, he breezed through the door, trashed. I had my phone set to record, just so I'd remember every single minute in therapy later (and forever when I tried to convince myself I could continue living there, or even continue being his friend). In the recording, I tell him this is for my therapist.

"Help her, therapist!" he laughed drunkenly into the phone.

"Where were you?" I asked.

"I told you, I was at the Sweetwater Festival with Chad," he said.

"Yeah, I recall," I said tersely. "You said you wanted to go to dinner to celebrate my graduation."

". . . yeah?"

"And then you didn't come back. And you were MIA until three in the morning with no word. Then you called, *at 3 a.m.* to ask me to pick you up," I recounted as if this justified my outrage.

"We didn't have sex. We only kissed," he said matter-of-factly.

"Then why did you invite me to dinner? Why did I rush to finish my paper? Why did I get dressed? To meet you for dinner. If you knew you weren't going to bother, why put me through all that?" I reasoned.

"I wasn't planning to not come back. *She was just more interesting than you,*" he said.

In the fullness of time, I can tell you why this happened. I was graduating from college, crossing my final hurdles for something that was statistically very unlikely in every way. And *I had made it.*

Because he is a narcissist, he had to put the attention back on himself. Reestablish his power over me. And he did that by spinning up an entire emotional circus right before finals. He fed off spinning me up and triggering my trauma. *It wasn't his fault; she was more interesting than me.*

He thought of himself as a real operator. Someone who was playing all his relationships as chess pieces to their greatest advantage to him.

But later he went to great effort and expense to hang his diploma on the wall weeks before I received mine to have it up alongside all my cool awards that my friends would often chat about when they came over. And while I was completely fine with it, it was a little transparent for "an operator," if I may say.

Todd also hit on my friends and badmouthed me to our mutual friends so much that it often got back to me.

The opposite of love isn't hate. It's indifference.

I was indifferent to his behavior. It made it much less fun for him, I'd imagine. Whenever I asked Todd why he said such awful things about me to our friends, he'd get mad at whoever had told me. The Bro Code had been violated! *That was the issue!*

Y'all, he was so surprised that his friend had told me while simultaneously being impressed that he'd "made a play" for me. Whatever. I was tired. I certainly wasn't feeling romantic toward Todd. He traveled for work and with his friends and was cheating all the time. He'd go on these role-playing websites and meet strangers and hook up with them on "work" trips. I didn't care. I was *way out* on that.

Worst of all, at my new weight and new "personal brand success" status, he had decided I was worthy of events with his parents. *Now.*

When you finally get recognition from people who felt like you were nothing, it's meaningless to you. Take that from me. If you're waiting for recognition from someone else, or you're working toward it, let it go. It won't be worth anything when you get it; it will taste like ash in your mouth. Unless you are letting the anger drive you toward greater things in your life, let it go. There is no "earning it." They just benefit from you believing that.

Validation doesn't come from other people; you can only get it from yourself.

Luckily for me, "becoming worthy of their respect" drove me to the top of college.

But his dad, Mr. Big, *stayed* unimpressed.

It's not me; it's you.

Toward the end of our time together Todd's family went on a family vacation to Florida over holiday break. Each kid brought a "friend." Todd brought me. We had been living together for five years at that point. I offered to pay my way, and it offended them, but also I had to do everything *their* way. I couldn't pay for anything or go anywhere not on the official itinerary. Todd's friend. A prop. I got one vacation a year that I had to save up for because I was a regular person, and I had to spend it as a prop of a medium-rich family. Worst trip ever.

Todd was turning thirty, and we went out for drinks with his parents to celebrate one of the nights. Still in awe of Mr. Big's "triumphing over adversity," I asked him, "So any advice for turning thirty?"

He peered down at me, clearly annoyed I'd spoken to him.

"What??"

"I said 'any advice for those of us getting closer to thirty?'" I shouted up to him, from apparently my lowly trash can house beneath his feet.

Mr. Big flared his nostrils. Then he looked me dead in the eye, and said, "Pfft. For you? No. Not at all. If I had achieved as little as you have by the time I was thirty, I would've killed myself." Then he walked off.

He must've been holding *that one* in for a long time because he had it in the chamber.

I stood there and let that sink in. If this was their respect, they could keep it.

And, trust me, it was.

I decided to shake it off and head over to the nearby dance floor full of older folks trying to dance to the music the DJ was playing.

As I walked over to the dance floor, I straightened my little black dress and held my head up. I immediately started making friends with all the older folks (because Florida in the winter) and taught them the Cupid Shuffle, as the O'Briens all sat stone-faced, having no fun. I didn't need to say what I was thinking; they got the message, I'm sure:

It's not me; it's you.

Trapped

One time I was at their house when the O'Brien's youngest daughter called to see whether she could stay out a little past curfew. Her mother couldn't decide on her own, so she brought the question to Mr. Big, interrupting his pontificating to his rarely seen son, Todd. Something about "Yahoos driving across the golf course"; I just tuned it out. I have *real* problems. Not champagne problems.

"Polly . . . ," he said disappointedly, muttering and shaking his head. Both of them went to join the daughter on the phone out of earshot of Todd and me.

"Why does he talk to her like that?" I asked Todd.

"Like what?" he asked, immediately defensive.

"Like . . . a dog who peed on the rug," I answered; repeating it to try to place the emphasis *"Polly . . ."*

"What do *you* know?" he sneered. "You want to compare freaking Karen . . . ?" He didn't need to finish the question, because certainly, no, I didn't mean to compare the O'Briens to the Smiths in terms of toxicity or abuse. But I also wanted to be clear that I did not need to be spoken to like I'd peed on the rug as a grown woman.

Whenever we were at his parents' house, Todd would sit near me and squeeze my thigh as hard as he could whenever I tried to speak in front of his parents. Anything that might challenge them at all, even if it put me in an obvious lie that I in no way had the skill to gracefully escape. It didn't matter to him—I wasn't a whole person.

I graduated from Georgia State with great friends, great experiences, and amazing references from my professors. I buttered up one professor with baked goods, the true greaser in academia, but they had all recommended me for employment. I was the student president of the department. I met Jane Goodall. Loudly. I was in all of the top student networking activities. I was in the Atlanta Independent Women's Network. I met civil rights activist John Lewis at networking events at which he was speaking, twice. I had job prospects.

And I was going to have to leave it all behind and start over just to survive Todd's swamp.

One of the deciding factors for me as to whether to keep living with him and being his friend occurred when he told me how proud of me he was:

"I'm the only one who ever believed in you and ever thought you'd amount to anything, and, *see*, I was right."

First, *I'm* the only one who believed in me.

And, second, *you sound like Karen, Todd . . .*

The relationship, which deteriorated into a friendship, had deteriorated beyond recognition. By that point, I knew he just wasn't capable of love.

Around the same time, I was swiftly coming to the conclusion that I wasn't going to find my dream job in Atlanta, which truly broke my heart because I loved (and still love) Atlanta. I'll always think of The A as my hometown.

In one of my last classes at Georgia State, the professor told us to write a letter to our future selves. She wanted us to write down all our hopes for the future, our dreams for ourselves. She was going to mail them to us at an undisclosed time. I wrote as much as I felt comfortable sharing just in case she opened them, but I didn't reveal the real truth in my heart:

I hope you're not still trapped.

Boston

In an effort to expand my options, I looked into job opportunities in Boston as well. It seemed there were way more biotech jobs there, and I was done with this whole situation. I was ready to burn it down just so I could move on. It should've been done years earlier, truthfully. So I packed all my stuff into a U-Haul and hit the road with my Chihuahua/Boston Terrier mix dog. It was scary but liberating.

Todd called fake-crying *constantly*, waiting for me to fail so I would come back. He left messages crying that I had "left and taken [his] home with [me]." His sister went to stay with him for a while. I was shocked he told her I'd left. I was shocked he cared that I'd left. In fact, I'd heard he was making his way around trying to sleep with anyone who knew me. (Unsuccessfully, *but still*, it felt bad.)

I honestly didn't want him to suffer regardless of all he had done to punish me for whatever was inside him. I just couldn't keep drowning to keep him afloat anymore. I wanted to live my own life rather than just be his life raft. And all he wanted was to have someone beneath him, keeping him above water. That wasn't at all what I was meant for. Maybe it was all I wanted for myself at one point, but I was certainly beyond that at that point.

I lost most of our mutual "friends" when I left him behind. I guess some of them felt like I should've supported him indefinitely, regardless of how he treated me. Those people weren't my friends, obviously, because friends don't expect a woman to bear the weight and social responsibility in any addiction in which her partner finds himself silently, indefinitely, and without complaint. No matter what he chooses. No matter what it costs her. Especially if he is a charming and intelligent narcissist.

Drown quietly.

The truth about abuse survivors is the same truth about everyone in relationships: we attract relationships in which we are comfortable. Not happy; comfortable. If your upbringing was toxic, you are comfortable in toxic relationships. If you were raised by a narcissist who lost the battle to dominate you to a cleverer narcissist, well then.

I thought I had won by leaving Karen behind; really, I just exchanged one prison for another. One set of rules for another. One abuser for another. *Out of the frying pan into the fire.*

My real friends were sad to see me go but totally okay with me leaving. They had watched the things he'd done over the years and had been begging me to stop being so blind, assuring me he wasn't even *my friend* anymore. And no one was happier to see me leave than Bob and Miss Jan. They'd been telling me to leave him since I spent Thanksgiving dinner with them in 2007 rather than being alone. That's the worst part of every ending, isn't it? I love them, but your hindsight is twenty/twenty, friends? Have mercy.

Now, I know what some of you are thinking: surely, he'll be pissed when he reads this and you'll have some problems. But as he well knows himself, this is *the very least* of it. He's getting off cheap. Like always.

He texted me one more time and sent me a final box of things I'd left behind, although my things were covered in rat droppings and animal urine and I had to throw them away. I mean, that wasn't subtle.

Todd: Hey.

Di: Hey . . . ?

Todd: How are you?

Di: Fine. What's up?

Todd: You got this letter in the mail here that didn't get forwarded to your new address.

Di: Okay?

Todd: Yeah, it's the weirdest thing because the envelope is in your handwriting.

I hope you're not still trapped, I remembered.

Di: Yeah. That was a stupid college project. You can just throw it out.

Todd: Okay cool, yeah, I figured it was like in the Nelson Mandela movie: "If she left it, she meant to throw it away."[67]

Di: Yep. Thanks.

Todd: Yep.

I hope you're not still trapped.

---

67 *Invictus*, directed by Clint Eastwood (Burbank, CA: Warner Bros. Pictures, 2009), DVD.

Level Setting

There is a unique feeling to surviving something or someone. I don't know a word for it. It's searing pain, as if something is being burned away from your soul through disinfectant and cauterization. It's also cold. The cold you get in places where you can be soaked all the way through to your bones with rain or snow, but the wind keeps blowing through you. It feels chaotic. It feels overcaffeinated.

Afraid to sleep. Afraid to bathe. Afraid to let down your guard.

It's like being asleep with your jeans and sneakers on for a while. Always ready to run. It can suffocate you and steal your breath; the fear of the unknown.

And you're *that* for a long time. But, in between, there are the briefest moments where you will feel the unmistakable giddiness of hope for your future. Where you will take a safe, free breath and know it for the blessing it is.

You'll start to know who you really are in those moments. When you go through them, they're painful. But when you survive them, *they level set* your life. There's nothing below that level that can ever "get you" again.

When I first escaped to Atlanta, I would lie awake at night listening to the trains moving stuff back and forth and feel very far away from the people who had hurt me. I'd listen to the crickets and the hum of the stifling heat and know that no one would ever hurt me like that again. And no one has raised an unanswered hand to me *since*.

When I left Atlanta, I was running from the life I'd thought I wanted. The life I had prayed for. But eventually the box grew too small. Like all boxes do. They aren't meant to be forever. That's not growth. Once you survive certain things, you know you can. And no one can take that from you. This is level setting. And it changes where you can fall to if you fail. That's power.

I knew I'd never be homeless again. Never be hungry again. And it's made all the difference.

The First Mother

I never wanted kids. I was so afraid that everything that had been done to me was waiting, crouching inside me like a spider. Actually, I thought that because adults explained to me over and over again that, while maybe we *could* agree that I "got out," there was **no way** my trauma wouldn't be handed down to my children.

As I look back, I wonder whether they availed themselves of that same caution they so kindly bestowed upon me. As I look around, I can see *they did not.*

I have been in therapy since I was removed from my mother. But a lot of people older than me think therapy is just "for crazy people." And that foolishness has led them to live very contentious and ultimately unexamined lives. And *unexamined* doesn't usually lead to "best" in my experience. Not for parenting or humaning.

I'm out here breaking generational curses and considering the work my soul has to do, and that's just not where some people are at. Some people pass down exactly what they hated about their own parents because they never did anything "drastic"—like therapy or other inner work—to break out of that well-worn path. So they stayed in that same path with those same behaviors. And then they are shocked when their kids hate them as much as they hated their parents. But it's the same trajectory. *The definition of insanity.*

When I first found out I was pregnant, my partner and I weren't married yet. Sorry, Kit. I was avoiding marriage for trauma reasons, but I was committed to my partner. We bought a house together within like six months of my being back in Boston, our bank accounts were linked, we had pets together, and we were living that queer, elder-millennial[68] lifestyle. Once we were pregnant, we kind of both looked at each other and were like *Wow, this needs to get serious real quick—we need to get the government involved!* I'm paraphrasing, obviously, but that was the overall feeling.

Pregnancy was awful for me. I hated every single moment of it. Sorry again, Kit. I felt weaker and more scared, right when I needed to be feeling powerful and more ready. There's no ready. They try to sell you "ready," but you can't buy "ready" at the store.

You can try it. I sure did.

"Ready" is another one of those abstract ideas that is mostly marketing. And it's subjective. Ready for motherhood. With (wait for it) the correct and best products. Which products are correct and best? Well, don't worry, they will let you know. And then you will be judged.

I kept up with that all the way through, I would say, the fourth trimester of my first child, Kit. Fourth trimester means the first three months after the baby is born where they are just a crying potato.

I could not understand why I was feeling so bad. Everything I had read seemed to be wrong for Kit. When I wasn't breastfeeding him, he was crying. I couldn't sleep. If I even handed him to someone else, he'd wail.

Then on the last night before we were due to depart the hospital, Jay, my partner, miraculously got Kit to sleep.

I remember waking up to a nurse standing over me. And this is after many days of insomnia. I'd just given birth, so take these quotes as *paraphrased* at best:

"Who are you?" I asked.

"I'm Nurse Jackie. I'm your overnight nurse. I'm here to check your vitals."

---

68 I say elder because we managed to find a house in the market. Again because of magic, I assume.

"Great, thanks."

"Are you breastfeeding him?" she asked, gesturing to Kit, who was asleep.

"I'm trying!" I said.

"I know you'll do great, honey," she said. Then she leaned in and said, "I probably shouldn't say this, but I feel compelled to tell you I lost an infant patient today."

I was thinking: I saw this on *House*. Is this like that time when all the infants got sick because of a candy striper? Is today the day my *House* knowledge saves us all? Finally? Vindication! *What, no one else??*

What I actually said was probably more of a panicked: "What?! How?"

"Well, again, and I don't know why I'm telling you—" she began.

"Skip that!" I instructed.

Too direct!

"I'm sorry?" she asked.

"I mean, please don't worry about it. That happens all the time. My grandmother told me it was my purpose on this earth, so please feel free to continue." I prattled through my usual comforting speech without much feeling because honestly, I'd just given birth. I hadn't yet even washed off the inexplicable Gorilla Glue they apparently use as tape to keep IVs in.

"Isn't that just the sweetest thing! The Lord works in such mysterious ways . . . " she began.

"Ma'am!" I interrupted, startling everyone within earshot and stupidly waking my human infant. He settled back in.

Thank you, Jesus.

Fully awake, I got out my Southern church whisper voice, which is really everyone's church whisper-rage voice (but they've really *perfected* it in Atlanta).

"Ma'am! I would love to hear about *all the ways* in which the Lord is mysterious, right after this. You were saying you had an infant patient die?!" I prompted, trying to soften the question midway through to get her to actually want to tell me.

"Oh!" she said. "Yes, of course! It really was so sad. His mama was co-sleeping him. She fell asleep, rolled over on him in her exhaustion, and suffocated him."

What?!

"I didn't even know that happened!" I said, the unspoken being, "as an anthropology student, who would've heard about exactly this kind of thing."

"It's so sad," she said. "Just promise me you'll never fall asleep holding that baby!"

"I won't!" I said.

She walked out and I never saw her again. But obviously I was now scared to death of falling asleep breastfeeding my infant who could not be removed from me without wailing.

Number one, after I had some coffee and time to think about it: In the first place, I blamed myself; people just unload their stuff on me. Then I got to thinking, when would this have happened? At the hospital? Wouldn't that tragedy have made the news? Even if the patient had been a newborn, the local moms would've known about it. I checked. Diligently. It's a small area. No one had ever heard of such a thing, and people remembered other tragedies when I asked in mom groups.

I checked the story because, number one, if it was real, maybe there was a reason she "accidentally" told me. Maybe universe messages. And, number two, if she didn't "accidentally" tell me, what might have prompted the share?

My best guess: she's really against co-sleeping and wanted to scare me. But that's how people treat new mothers. I wasn't even specifically "for" or "against" co-sleeping at the time. I'm a little more culturally sensitive and, hopefully, more supportive of mothers than to judge one way or another. *You're doing great, moms. Just reminding you, you left your coffee in the microwave, again. I know! It's awful. I do it too.*

But as the pieces of the person I was before I was a mother to this human fell away, I mourned them. I grieved the loss.

I was depressed.

I wasn't sure how much until I was writing this. Kit had colic, and we didn't even know it until our second child, Artemis. Because you don't know. Kit had two settings: crying or eating. I was exhausted. There are thousands of books, blogs, articles, and well-intentioned advice givers to choose from. But they don't tell you anything about the specific issues that might come up with the specific type of human you have. At the end of the day, it's on you to figure out what kind of human you have. They tell you with kids that you get a blank slate to program, but really they come out fully coded. I think of it like a really serious video game that has levels.

I called down to the nurse on the day I was scheduled to go home from the hospital and asked for permission to leave.

"They just let me bring this kid out of here with no adult checking me?" I asked, incredulous.

She goes, "You brought it in here!" and then laughed hysterically.

"So . . . I can go then?"

"Yes. You can just go. Once you see the doctor, you can just go. But let us know so we can send a wheelchair. Hospital policy, you know! Everyone leaves in a wheelchair!" she said cheerily.

Lord, have mercy.

"So I guess I need to call you before leaving then?" I asked.

"Yes. Call us before you're leaving," she said, trying to hang up again.

"Wait!" I cried, giving up on being polite, tired, *and* neurodivergent. "Can that call be now?"

"Are you leaving now?" she asked.

"Yes, thank you, that's what I meant. Can I just leave with this kid or is there something else I need to do?" I asked.

"Oh, well, we'll send over your wheelchair!" she said before hanging up.

Cool.

When you become a mother, there's an identity tied to that. It overwrites everything you've written in your story. Maybe it's patriarchy, maybe it's marketing, but really it's an identity perception. Another frame of reference. But for all our blustering about how we support mothers and our values, *we definitely don't support mothers*. Not at all.

The way we talk about mothers puts them up on a pedestal as people reflect on their own dear mother, usually with rose-colored glasses. But it's an identity that often lessens a person's estimation of you.

"You're a superhero! I don't know how you do it!"

"Actually, we're struggling pretty hard over here in this pandemic, is there any way you could . . ."

"Parents and teachers should have a statue in town square! I support you!"

Cool. I've got it. Drown quietly.

As I tried to find my identity in motherhood, I started where all neurodivergent people start: Hyperfocus! Knowing everything about babies will solve this! Parenting groups! Parenting hobbies!

But as the days went by, I got more and more depressed because I felt like my partner could still leave for work, but I was home with Kit. Kit is an amazing kid, but being home alone with a colicky newborn when you can't sleep or shower is incredibly destabilizing.

Hyperfocusing while imagining all of the worst-case scenarios in advance and then planning for them so there are no variables has always been my go-to in solving new problems. For motherhood, trying to control all the outcomes was a super bad, trauma-induced solution.

All of the things I used to identify who I was before then—largely tied to my career and accomplishments—no longer defined me.

In an effort to keep some of my identity, I started little work projects. Starting to work on things I cared about and actually talking to people made me feel more like myself. I started doing more things that I was passionate about and eventually started a licensed staffing agency. Then a consulting practice.

I would say it was then that I found the most joy in being a mother. After that, I had to find myself in it. Once I was able to tear away the things that didn't matter to discover the ones that did, I was able to make real friends in the mom community. But the only way I could do that was to also keep my brain tinkering on other adult problems.

When Kit was two, we had Artemis. Our dedicated Leo. Artemis was due the first week in September, and I was already starting to have back cramps at thirty-eight weeks. I called my OB and spoke to the nurse.

"You're thirty-eight weeks?" she asked.

"Yes," I said through gritted teeth.

"Okay, Mama, why don't you go take a shower? It's probably cramps. Call me later!" she advised.

I stopped my partner who was on his way to work.

"I need you to stay here," I said. "I feel really weird. Can you call your mom to watch Kit?"

"What? Yeah. I can. But remember it's my sister Rhonda's birthday; they're probably busy?" he said.

"What? Yeah. Whenever she can. I have to take a shower," I said, limping to our shower as he got his mother on the phone.

Just then, my water unexpectedly broke.

"Di?" he called to me. "Mom wants to know how fast you need her. She's getting green tea with Rhonda."

"My water broke," I said.

"WHAT?!" he said, throwing open the shower door, while on the phone with his mom.

"I SAID MY WATER BROKE. So *immediately* would be great."

He relayed the information to his mother who apparently beamed herself to us from the next town over.

"Okay, update," I wheezed to Jay. "I can't walk and I need help getting some pants on. And we should drive to the hospital immediately. This is happening too fast."

We sped safely to the hospital in the Fit, years of video games having prepared Jay for this moment. The Fit is a terrible car to be going into labor in. You have no room, and you feel every single bump. Fortunately we live close.

Jay pulled into the hospital's parking lot, and I wheezed my way out of the front seat.

"*Nope*," said my body.

"I can't walk," I said when he got to me.

"Well, here, lean on me," he said.

But I couldn't stand. I was in too much pain to walk.

"Get back in the car, and drive me to the front!" I shrieked.

He did and we put the car in park in the unloading station. Jay grabbed someone's empty nearby wheelchair and put me in it.

"What should I do with the car?" he wondered aloud.

"LEAVE IT!"

Fortunately, they had a valet we didn't know about. He was like, "No, definitely, good luck," as we just left the car and keys with him and ran off.

I was in screaming agony.

As Jay *ran* me past the front desk, they just cheered him on and shouted directions:

"Third floor, Daddy!" they said, laughing.

I hate everyone.

We weren't in the elevator alone, but it was a doctor who was laughing at my screams.

"Congratulations," he said with a chuckle, getting off on the second floor.

Fortunately, my partner wasn't laughing. This hadn't happened last time.

As we pulled up to the maternity desk, I tried to check in.

"Spell your name for me again," she shouted at Jay over me.

"C-I-R-U-O-L-O," he recited.

"L-L-O?" she asked. "I can't find it . . ."

I began to hysterically laugh. That's always what people hear. I have no idea why. No matter who you say it to or how slowly you say it. People repeat back "L-L-O."

Finally she let us into an open maternity room. A nurse met us at the door because I was still screaming.

"Hi, Mama," she said. "I need you to calm down, okay? Is this your first?" She began rubbing my back.

I vehemently shook my head no because I could no longer speak.

"Okay, let's get you up on the bed," she said. "Take your sweats off."

By the way, in movies when your water breaks, there's a puddle on the floor and that's it. In real life when your water breaks, you leak amniotic fluid like you're peeing yourself the entire birth. I get why they didn't tell me the truth, but I'm telling you the truth. My water broke both times naturally before birth. Same thing happened both times. Now you won't be surprised if you're like me.

I climbed on top of the bed as instructed because neurodivergent people have a high pain tolerance. But then I couldn't move again once I got on my back.

The nurse asked when I last ate.

"Please, help!" I panted.

She continued with her questions, ignoring me.

"Please, help!" I said to Jay, pointing to the nurse.

She started again.

"Look," Jay interrupted. "'Help' is a four letter word to this woman; if she's asking *you* for help, she's f——g dying!"

The nurse, to her credit, listened to that.

"Let me check," she said and started to check how dilated I was.

"Okay," she said. "I'm just going to hit this alarm right here. Everything is fine."

She sounded an alarm across the floor.

"You were right, Mama. I can feel this baby's head," she said.

I literally hate when people won't listen to me because I'm a woman. Bring a man to every medical interaction. I swear to God.

When Artemis was born, her umbilical cord was wrapped around her neck three times. After Artemis was clearly no longer in danger, the doctors, med students, and nurses loudly came in and discussed how they'd never seen such a long umbilical cord, how it had been wrapped around her neck three times. They thought it was cool that my body knew that if she were in there any longer we'd have both not made it and that it needed to give birth to her two weeks early. She looked at me with her eyes open, while listening to the sounds of the room.

Jay called his mother to tell her Artemis had been born.

It was still Jay's sister Rhonda's[69] twenty-first birthday. Rhonda and Artemis were born on the same day. Artemis was born two weeks early, making her

---

69 Rhonda picked her own fake name.

a Leo baby. I gave her a name that meant "grace on fire" after how I'd always felt about the gifts my Nana Santos had given me. And I wasn't wrong.

I tell you this birth story first because my story with Kit was so different. It took me twenty hours from the time my water broke to give birth to Kit. And he was nearly a week late. He just wanted no part of it.

They're both still exactly that way. She's kicking doors down, and him, you have to convince.

Kit was due from mid to late May, and my nurse was booking me for a C-section for June 7 "to guard against the devil," she said. My nurse was super legit, by the way. She had that "I love you, now get it together because you've got this" energy I really respond to.

But on May 31 at 1 p.m., I had just ordered a really yummy lunch for myself when my water broke. It feels like a water balloon breaking in your body. Like a snapped rubber band. And, as I said, the water does not stop rushing out of you.

Motherhood is an exercise in letting go of the illusion of control. But control helped me feel safe, so that exercise was not my favorite life level.

We called the on-call OB-GYN group because it was a Sunday, and they wanted us to come in because my water had broken.

"Are you sure it isn't just pee?" the nurse asked when I first called to report my situation to them. "How can you be sure?"

"Are you serious? Who could mistake this for pee? Is something *serious* happening to me? There is water running out of my body!" I was frantic.

Medical professionals seem to either always assume I am stupid, or always assume women are stupid, and I can't be sure which from my experience. *Por qué no los dos,*[70] *amiright?*

"Okay great," she answered. "Just making sure. Why don't you go to the hospital, check in, and let them know we're worried about infection because your water broke."

---

70 Why not both?

"Perfect," I hung up. Turning to Jay, I said, "My water broke and they want me to go to the hospital because they're worried about infection."

Jay has this mode that we in his family call Bear Mode. It's what it sounds like.

He was a whirl of motion grabbing everything and putting down a towel for the aforementioned not-pee.

When we got to the hospital, we were checked into maternity.

"You need to dilate to at least ten centimeters before the baby can be born," they said. "You'll need to walk him out."

I wanted to have Kit naturally. I wanted a no intervention, no drama, "my body can handle this" birth. By 6 p.m., I was in active labor.

The pain from labor is so horrible that I vomited in front of Jay. Several times.

Okay, maybe just a few interventions!

When the anesthesiologist arrived, he had Jay hold up my hospital gown because I was shivering with pain and adrenaline.

"Hey! I've seen this tattoo before! A lot, actually!" he said.

"No you haven't," I said through chattering teeth. "A friend of mine designed it for me before he died to remind me I'm my own body and no one else can claim it. It's one of a kind."

"Everyone thinks they have a one-of-a-kind tattoo, hon," he retorted.

"I think I'm going to kill you," I said.

He laughed.

"Yeah, that's my whole thing with moms who have tattoos: it gets them mad and they don't notice the epidural needle," he said.

"I didn't enjoy it," I said. *In full labor.*

"Did you notice the huge needle?" he asked.

"No,"

"Well, that's the point!"

"I'm not enjoying this. Is this over?"

"Thank you, folks, I'll be here all week!" he said, spinning off his chair and rushing out the door.

Cute, huh?!

I labored for Kit for twenty hours. In the end, I didn't need to get ten centimeters dilation. I needed to get to at least twelve centimeters. Because his head was fourteen centimeters.

As my OB-GYN dumped "all the oil" on my bits to try to get Kit out, someone asked me whether I wanted a full-length mirror.

"FOR WHAT?!" I roared, incredulous.

"Some parents like to watch their child be born in the mirror," my super chill doctor reported.

Much too chill.

"GET THE KID OUT OF ME! I DON'T WANT TO WATCH!"

This was not my day to be a hero.

I didn't want to elongate the nearly indescribable agony of a bigger-than-average head in my smaller-than-average pelvic cradle, literally tearing the two halves of my pelvis away from each other, to wait for them to find a mirror for me to watch his head come out. You can miss me with that.

My message was received.

Kit was born on June 1. The day after my water broke.

And because of that, I thought all the births we saw on TV were lies.

After Kit, I told a lot of childless friends that those "Oops! My water neatly broke!" stories, the screaming, and the highly dramatized rush to the hospital "Hollywood birth stories" were just that. Stories for drama. And I was scared to go through that and thought maybe other parents would be scared as well. I thought maybe people should know it can take a long time. It turns out all birth stories are different. Between my two kids, one took twenty hours, the other took twenty minutes. Same mother. Who knows? Not me.

My bad, Hollywood.

Thanks for the check, Life.

But I would say the thing that has impacted my motherhood story the most so far has undoubtedly been the COVID-19 pandemic.

Kit was four when this started and Artemis was two. I could keep them entertained and semi-educated with interactive events and crafts for a while. But

I also worked. The scariest part of being me in this pandemic was how much epidemiology goes into a biological anthropology degree. I spent most days trying not to let my brain spin out into "worst-case scenario plus two kids" mode.

Over three million women in the United States left the workforce to take up primary caregiver responsibilities. I knew I couldn't do only that and, fortunately, or unfortunately, kept working.

I work in diversity, equity, belonging, and inclusion, and we just became workforce social workers contextualizing racial social justice movements, misogyny, and every other thing. It kept my brain engaged, but it also sucked every breath from my lungs. I would text my friends who do what I do in different spaces and ask them how things were at their end of the battlefield. (Their replies were that it was not good at their end, either.)

In the fall of 2020, Kit was doing kindergarten virtually. He had a great teacher. We were very lucky. But early on in his interactions with other kids his age, I noticed he had some different things going on. He hated loud noises. Deep voices. He immediately thought every correction anyone made about his behavior meant someone hated him. He didn't seem to be maturing in the same way as other kids.

Hmm . . . not quite just ADHD, but on this spectrum . . . I thought.

I spoke to a lot of childhood professionals and they agreed he was probably a little stunted by the pandemic but, ultimately, he was developing fine.

He had a frontal lisp from the time he was born. By the time Artemis was three, I could tell she didn't have one, so I worried and noted it to professionals around him. But we were in a pandemic. I couldn't just get him seen by a doctor unless something was wrong.

By the time Kit went to first grade, we were back to masks in person, locally, and he hadn't been in a non-preschool classroom yet. As a child with neurodiversity.

Within weeks, his teacher reached out to me to let me know I should have Kit assessed so we could get more support at school. I got all the paperwork to all the proper authorities, but, again, we were in a pandemic and no one could help. I was on every waitlist for a private professional assessment, which they wanted four to six thousand dollars for. I was leaving messages every week for every child psychologist in town, and they weren't returning my calls. Because they were super overwhelmed.

What were they doing for people who had less access than I had with potentially more serious situations? I thought about it a lot.

Finally, in February, Kit was involved in a situation with another child and had to sit in the office all day. He was six. Not his fault. He got overstimulated and just acted without thinking. But it scared me to death thinking that could just happen without the right support.

The support I couldn't find for him.

Finally, after months of searching, plus some magic, we found someone who walked us through the process of demanding the school test Kit for an individualized education program (IEP). Because he was clearly going to need extra help for the foreseeable future.

Kit's teacher is awesome. We've been lucky. Everyone involved was great. But ultimately their hands were tied. He has a high IQ and struggles a lot to connect with the material in a group with a lot going on. It didn't warrant a true IEP. But he will continue to need interventions and special support to perform at school like the other kids.

I wasn't surprised by any of these outcomes having already gone through many similar conversations when trying to seek help for myself. I'd had to get myself a tutor to learn concepts that I didn't understand already.

To the credit of the school, they've put a lot of things in place for him to help that I never had, and I'm really grateful. The awareness of neurodiversity has come a long way since I was a kid. Not all the way to helping each child reach their individual maximum potential, but medium. It's not really the teachers; it's the underfunded system. These days, Kit is learning how to regulate himself and take himself out of overstimulating situations when he can control it. I'm proud of him.

But fighting for him has been super triggering for me. It's a great school, and it took me months to leave him there without crying. Jay had to start driving him for a while.

Now we all walk over and know the local walking neighbors.

Artemis will have no such problems fitting in. She's a tiny me. She developed a very Leo attitude that we are all here to serve her sometime last year. I remember when I realized it. We had gotten an ice cream from the ice cream truck, and she dropped a small part of it that fell on the grass. Totally salvageable, in my opinion. But she threw her arms in the air and went full "woe is me!" Could not even. At four.

I'll be fine, but send coffee.

We're getting there. I sometimes ask people with kids who are older than ours if it ever gets easier.

"Easier?" a mom laughed. "I wouldn't say it gets easier. 'Little kids little problems, big kids big problems.' But you *do* sort of 'Level-Up.'"

In my experience, that frame of reference works: Basically, you get all the way to the boss level, fail many times at beating it, and then finally persevere (or not), only to find the next level has a new boss. And that whole time? You are dealing with your own trauma from that level. *Or not.*

But you're being presented with it. You're being reminded of it. You're being triggered by it. It's your job as a parent to decide how you overcome that.

Because once you're an adult, *you* get to decide what that means.

Motivations

I'm reading Glennon Doyle's book *Untamed* because my work-wife has been trying to get me into her forever and I'm always slow to warm up to suggestions like that from folks.

Why, Di?

Because a lot of the time, with some of these folks (not Glennon—I love Glennon—but *some* of these lifestyle brands), you gotta be able to have that lifestyle before you can live your "authentic" self, which is really just capitalism and not best for humans. It's not authentic. It's marketing—and not doable for the other million percent of us who weren't born like that.

Now, authenticity isn't a dirty word in my mind. In fact, I think people learning about themselves, drinking their water, going to therapy, and taking their meds[71] are all great. I am here for the mental health revolution.

But I am *not* here for the Instagram story of the mental health revolution, *which will be viewed from a specific but majority view. Also, buy these meds for what you have.* Commodified human existence.

I'm just going to speak broadly for the human race here. I'm feeling really confident on this one: We don't want our mental health and our agency to seek it within ourselves removed from us and then marketed back as some

---

71   Coffee isn't meds. Believe me, I've tried it. So far zero therapists and only one enabling
     friend have gone for that.

abstract idea one might one day obtain through paid "gurus," experts, and medication, but only if you have the money for it because the system wasn't built for everyone. Like "fitness."

Don't come for me about "fitness" unless you *also* had to write a college research paper on food deserts, driving from Kroger to Kroger in the spring heat[72] of Atlanta, measuring the distance between stores where people could buy fresh produce and how they would get there and what the cost differences are between stores versus gas stations and bodegas not specifically known for their produce. Because I did that. "Food deserts." Google it.

Health and fitness are not the pinnacle of human existence, and you might consider the people living with chronic conditions for whom health would never be possible when you say that. I am exhausted by the idea of measuring my personal body's fitness by other people's set standards. I was "obese" when I was running marathons. So I lost more weight. Did you know the body mass index wasn't created on or for women's bodies? Yeah. Check it out.

A doctor finally caught me at 130 lb. with Todd telling me he thought I'd look better at 120 lb. The doctor, who was a Black woman, sat me down and told me: "BMI isn't for women. They didn't even include us in the data sampling for the research. Standardizing *for* white men and *by* white men will kill you. *Only **they** think their experience is universal.*"

"With everything you've got on," she said, gesturing to my boobs, "you should never be lower than 137 lb."

I stayed at that practice for the entire time I was in Atlanta. Todd had gaslit me into an eating disorder that year so, coupled with my experience with food trauma, she very likely saved my life.

To paraphrase a quote I once heard, I believe, from Megan Rapinoe, the only thing a woman shouldn't wear after thirty is the weight of other people's expectations.

Which brings my ADHD back around to me avoiding Glennon Doyle's work just in case it was another "women's lifestyle brand."

---

72 I know. It's the humidity that kills you. Not the 95 degrees. Good note.

One thing I hate more than lifestyle brands that say one thing and do another is lifestyle brands that use religion as a method of control and manipulation to say one thing and do another. Harming women for God. Speaking for God. And sometimes I let that cloud my judgment because as Lafayette Reynolds[73] once perfectly said: "Jesus and I agreed to see other people, but that don't mean we don't still talk from time to time."

I have no beef with Jesus, to be clear. I am a big fan. *I love Christians.* Two of our Christian friends brought us vegan meals for a week when Artemis was born early and I was recovering. My local mom community did the same. *Real* Christians. I am less of a fan of people who weaponize *their* religions to control the lives of others in secular states. It's all kind of the same argument about standardization of the human experience toward intentionally unattainable goals, to my mind. While not holding themselves to that same standard, obviously. That's against *my* religion.

Speaking of my religion; I am mostly a hodgepodge of beliefs based in my love of humanity. I read the entire King James Bible cover to cover several times when I was eleven before getting up the courage to ask Sister Agnes about some of the questions I had about Catholicism. I was getting First Communion at the time.

Now, if you are wondering why I was going through this process at age eleven, it was because Karen decided I needed to be baptized and that I was going to get caught up to my peers' catechism education in her church. Now, if it was only about bringing me into her church because she was such a good Catholic, as she would have everyone believe, we could've done that privately. However, it was about the community ceremony I neither wanted nor asked for.

But Karen said anything less than complete compliance to her dream of my being paraded around the church in front of the community was in defiance of her will and would not be tolerated.

Putting me in this position would grant her mass adoration at her church. But to her church, she insisted that my not being included

---

73 RIP Nelsan Ellis. Too good for this world.

and treated the same as the other children in this was tantamount to descrimination.

So the church put obstacles in her way. They insisted I be tutored by Sister Agnes. Sister Agnes was hardcore. Whenever Karen bragged to someone local about how I was being tutored in Catholicism by Sister Agnes personally, each expressed horror that she was still working with children. I begged not to. Sister Agnes smoked cigarettes while we watched movies about Jesus and read from the King James Bible—for months. And Karen told everyone I wanted to be a nun.

My name was included in the First Communion event flyer with the six-year-olds. Some really great townie parents laughed about my "needing to be baptized" to their kids. Of course, then their kids repeated that back to me.

It was a very small town, and everyone knew who the one foster kid no one wanted there was, so I was a little notorious. The weight of being known as "that kind of different," the kind of different that had never and would never touch most of the people in that town weighed on me daily.

Which brings me back to authenticity.

My authenticity comes from a place of trauma, of having everything that the human mind develops to keep itself safe ripped away. One-third of people who go through this kind of trauma become overachievers, and yet I'm one of the only foster kids I know of. Why is that? Is it because the math is wrong? No, it's because living life every day in the worst moments of your life is exhausting and traumatic. So we don't talk about it. People shouldn't be held responsible for the fact that my brain just works differently. And, more importantly, people shouldn't be held to the same standard.

One of the things that comes from some of these "toxic positivity" lifestyle brands is the idea that "anyone can do it if they try hard enough." If you aren't as happy as you could be, if you aren't successful, if you're suffering, it's your fault. *The Bootstraps Narrative.*

By the way, did you know the expression is not "pull yourself up by your bootstraps"? It was originally intended to describe an absurdist position like "you can't pull yourself over a fence by your bootstraps." I guess it still describes an absurdist position.

When I was a teenager, Karen got me involved in speaking engagements for foster parent training organizations. I'd tell my story and then grown adults would stand to ask me a question, often weeping uncontrollably at the story I had told. Then I would need to prop them up emotionally while they asked questions about how to assimilate foster children into their families.

These precious adults were people who had not examined their own traumas, their own childhoods, their own Madre Wounds. I'm not knocking them, to be clear, especially now that I'm an adult. "Adult me" is fine with questions from adults. "Child me" just wanted to be normal. It made it very obvious to me that not everyone was dealing with what I was dealing with. Often people were using me and other abuse survivors for what I call *trauma voyeurism*—to feel the unimaginable pain of what the survivor was feeling for a moment but then go back to their lives.

I started noticing people doing this with me way too late. It's a choose your own adventure for me, and it goes like this: I tell someone that I grew up in foster care. And too often they say something to the effect of, "Well, it's great to know that there are still good foster homes!"

I have three choices at that moment: (1) I can lie and exit the conversation ASAP. That's usually the easiest, and I don't like to shame people. (2) I can tell them I didn't grow up in a good foster home and then hurry to explain that I take their assumption as a compliment to spare their feelings (I don't). Or (3) I can ask them aloud why they've assumed I came from a good foster home and let them explain it. If I take option 2, I have to close the gap of why someone thinks that I come from a good foster home for them, and in option 3, I let them do it. Yeah, it's not great.

When I do tell them I didn't grow up in "one of the good ones," I usually have to infodump an overshare onto them. And that usually leaves them to rebalance with a platitude, something that everyone says that no one believes or examines.

"Well, if *you* can do it, anyone can!"

At first I laughed, agreed, and didn't see the harm in it. I used to feel relieved. *Great, now that that's over maybe we can talk about my actual interests.*

As I got older, I realized I might be the only foster kid any of them ever meet, and I can't let them get away and go off into the world thinking that's correct.

Number one: that's not a compliment.

Number two: Really? You look at me, you look at my face and think, *If she can do it, anyone can*? I worked thirty to fifty hours a week while I put myself through college on Tuesdays and Thursdays, five classes per semester. I was in every networking organization. Every. And then when I got out of college, I still had *no* network I could use to get myself a job.

And then someone will assume everyone is like me. Anyone can survive foster care. No. They can't. *And they don't.* We're letting ill-intentioned politicians change the narrative around this to suit their own agendas. I'm here because *I'm* magic, not because the system works.

It does not.

It's like the illusory narrative that every person in the United States can start with no money and become whatever they want. Does it happen for some people? Apparently. I love The Rock. Which of the people who claim "people just need to pull themselves up by their bootstraps" is The Rock? Oh, no one?

My point is this: I'm here to tell you that I am not the exception that proves the rule. The rule proves that I am the exception. I am exceptional.

But there are nearly half a million kids in the US foster care system as we speak. It shouldn't just be the exceptional who survive.

Who is responsible for foster kids if not the system? We are. We adults. We are responsible for making changes, for funding programs. We need to stop pretending that some children are worth less than our own children because they were born to others.

Trust me, it can be everyone's responsibility now or it can be everyone's future later. The problem doesn't go away just because we'd rather not deal with it. Or because we don't know how to. We're better than this as human beings. Children deserve better. We need to account for our own traumas to build community.

Let's put in the research, put in the money, put in the work, and grow the future we want. Instead of hiding from a future we're afraid of.

It's up to us. Right now.

Insider/Outsider

The Boston area is really tech/biotech heavy because of the saturation of great schools. When I first started consulting for local companies, I felt the pressure to prove myself in a new industry. I took on a lot of clients. I didn't need to because I could afford to be more selective at that point. But, due to trauma, it took me a long time to find the right balance, so I'd just keep taking on more and more clients because of the pressure I put on myself. They'd offer less than my hourly rate and I'd take it "for the exposure." *I know.* But I built a pretty great client base that way.

Whenever I'd get a call to handle a DEI[74] project, there was already an ongoing issue. Then that CEO would connect me to the next friend he had who was facing a similar problem and off I'd go to the next fire.

As a result of that kind of "fixer" role, work was hard but abundant. I worked with companies across the world on DEI issues that were impacting their workforce. I learned an incredible amount about humans all over the world and how each interaction might play out based on cultural identities.

Did you know usually only Americans will raise their hand at an international talk, even if the speaker asks whether anyone has questions? Isn't that fascinating?

---

74 Diversity, Equity, Inclusion.

The frontline of the conversation on racial equity is happening within the US. As bad as it is, as terrible as we are at it, at least we're having the conversation.

Indeed, I was leading a conversation with a team in Europe, and a British woman asked me, in general, why are Americans so proud about being first generation or second generation? I began by relating the question to my own experience when a young man interrupted me.

"Di, if I may, I think her question is even simpler than that," he said. "Here in the UK, people have been citizens of this country for generation upon generation. Their families go back centuries sometimes. It's not like that for the Yanks. They can be born there after their family is from somewhere else."

"Oh!" she said.

"Oh," I said. "So you weren't actually asking me why we're proud, you were asking what 'first generation' is."

"Right," she said.

"Right," I replied.

And maybe five minutes later, a report came out in the UK declaring the country essentially, "not racist." The place that basically invented and exported white supremacy. But if you read the actual study that's not what it says. At all. In fact, the report says there are significant barriers to entry that were observed by the study, but that it's best not to discuss or delve into them too seriously so as to not "alienate" the good people on the center right.[75]

I asked several Black friends who left the US and lived somewhere else what their experience was, and many framed it like this: Other places seem to be more racist even though the racism isn't branded as such. It's more "baked in." America's racism is angrier and on purpose. But in other places, it's actually worse because it's *completely* unexamined. Racism is the accepted narrative.

---

75   The precise quote is: "However, we also have to ask whether a narrative that claims nothing has changed for the better, and that the dominant feature of our society is institutional racism and White privilege, will achieve anything beyond alienating the decent centre ground – a centre ground which is occupied by people of all races and ethnicities." Commission on Race and Ethnic Disparities, "Commission on Race and Ethnic Disparities: The Report," GOV.UK, March 2021, https://assets.publishing.service.gov.uk/government/uploads/system/uploads/attachment_data/file/974507/20210331_-_CRED_Report_-_FINAL_-_Web_Accessible.pdf.

In 2019, I decided I wanted to write a book[76] as a level zero educational tool for the projects I was taking on. Often, when I'd meet with a CEO or leadership team, he or they would be repeating the same five fake stories we tell ourselves about equity work.

I'd walk into an all-white, all-male room, and there would be a series of "things we are telling ourselves" about why things aren't "where we want them to be." Firstly, that all the women have left the company before reaching leadership positions not due to any toxic issues within the company but rather as a result of "having babies."

No, seriously.

Birth rates are going down. More women than men are graduating with computer science degrees, among other programs. And, somehow, we can't even take the next step in rational thought beyond what we've been told, especially when that something is a stereotype about a group to which we don't belong. It's wild. Any woman in tech will tell you. They don't want us there. It's she elephant in the room. But that's not what they say. They say we work until we have babies and then leave.

"There just aren't enough qualified women or people of color in the hiring pool," people would tell me. And when I asked what they had iterated on in regard to closing that gap, I was often met with blank stares.

"Oh, okay, so are you thinking of doing more types of outreach with coding classes or working with local schools on getting access to proper computers for students to learn on or something?" I'd ask, just as one example.

"What? No," they'd say. "We just told you what the problem was."

"Right . . . " I'd say.

"Right," they'd agree.

"But if you know what the problem is, why aren't you trying to solve it?" I'd ask.

"Because that's not our problem; that's an education problem! That's a system-level problem!" they'd argue.

---

76   Di Ciruolo, *Ally Up: The Definitive Guide to Building More Inclusive, Innovative and Productive Teams* (NY: Morgan James Publishing, 2021).

"Okay, but also if you want to keep growing at the rate you want to, I'm not sure how you aren't barrelling toward a huge staffing issue given the attrition you anticipate."

"Well, if *we* are, then everyone else is too! Because I don't know what [so and so] told you, but their DEI program is a joke. It is 100 percent marketing. That's why he put "marketing expert" in the job description! Because what good is it doing this type of thing if people don't see you doing it??"

". . . well, I think the work itself has inherent value to the people it helps, certainly," I'd try.

"Come on! Don't make *me* the bad guy here!" they'd say.

"Of course. Let me try again. What data do you have that tells you the problem with your leadership pipeline is that women are leaving your workforce to become stay-at-home parents?"

"What do you mean?" they'd say.

"I'm sorry, let me rephrase the question," I'd say. "What makes you think that there are no women on your leadership team or board because women are leaving to become stay-at-home mothers?"

The first man would inevitably stare at the faces of two other men—all in jeans and T-shirts by the way and wearing what I'm pretty sure were $800 sneakers. I'm not judging; I'm just saying.

"What do you mean 'how do I know?' *Everyone* knows that!" they'd sputter. "Right guys?!"

"Right!"

I can't even tell you exactly how it really went because it's NDA-protected but, trust me when I tell you, this was much cleaner than what is often actually said behind closed doors on the matter. Plus I left all the slurs out.

So what does this mean? Generally, it means the people who actually come to see me to change things aren't actually the people with the power to change things.

In fact, the people I spoke with the most post-2020 were Black and Brown people, especially women and queer people looking for advice on how to talk to their teams about making their workplaces more equitable and safer for *themselves*. Because it may shock you to find out that non-white people aren't born with critical race theory and or intersectional feminism downloaded into our brains. Plus we're taught the opposite. We run into these societal boundaries (while having people who aren't experiencing any boundaries tell us *there are no boundaries*). And if they are there? Well, that's just because you didn't work hard enough to overcome them, right?

It will usually become obvious from a life of living in your skin as a person who isn't white, a man, straight, Christian (or any of the above), that teaching systemic inequity to people who aren't always interested in learning it or, worst of all, are there for the wrong reasons, is a really specific skill you build.

Being able to divorce yourself from the situation as you argue for your own humanity is a really hard skin to develop. And, trust me, mine comes specifically through a life of trauma and like thirty years of therapy. It's a high price.

But I am fueled by a cold rage.

I am often asked in podcasts and interviews what advice I would give to people breaking in to DEI and, honestly, it's the same advice I have for anyone about breaking into tech: Do it for your own reasons. And know what those reasons are because nothing else will sustain you through the fight if you aren't *called* to it. There's no praise you will ever receive, no validation that will ever come, no money that will ever be enough if you aren't called to it because the system is bigger than you. And until we all decide we don't want this anymore, it *always* will be. But there will be moments, flashes really, where you will be part of something spectacularly human. And either that is enough to sustain you or you quit and go into business for yourself, with many going into the wellness industry. I've also seen a lot of "makers" come out of the system.

To some degree, any of us with any understanding of our job, and any *true* understanding of systemic oppression realize we are part of the system too. And our work can often specifically help the system do its worst because we can often make a place look *safer* than it is.

When I left my last job in tech to write *this* book, a friend of mine, a Black man, was devastated.

"I didn't think I belonged here in tech, and I was ready to quit until I met you. Please don't stay away long!" he wrote to me.

And, while I am truly honored, I am also worried that I don't take that seriously enough. If I am at a business, I might be used as someone who they say is there "to address issues" (which they don't actually plan to fix).

DEI leaders can be like shark netting that's built from the top down. I make the water look safer faster than it may in fact be. That can be harmful. So one of the first things I accepted about this line of work is that "not all money is good money."

I absolutely love my job. I still think there are great people in tech who are fighting to make tech what we know it can be. And I will continue to join them in that fight. But being a pandemic cruise director steering people ops teams through the Equity Awakening of 2020 has been unspeakably taxing.

Once a guy who attended one of my talks reached out to me later on LinkedIn. He made some racist comments at me—like they do—and, as I tried to explain and offer examples of why he was wrong, he said something I won't forget:

"What makes you think I don't understand?" he said.

That stopped me.

"What?" I asked.

"I said, 'What makes you think I don't understand?'"

"Because you're a racist?"

"*Yes*," he said. "What makes *you* think *I* don't understand, is what I'm asking."

What made me think that a racist person was ignorant? This racist person was very educated. He just decided that racism was the way he wanted to go. It gave him *power*.

Some people aren't racist because they're uneducated. The opposite also applies. Some people are very aware of the harm they do. And they enjoy it. It makes them feel powerful. And that's an important reality I almost never looked at.

Some people hurt people on purpose. It makes them feel good. Treat them accordingly.

Look What You Made Me Do

I've heard this from abusers for all of my life.

Karen said it whenever she left a mark. Or when she'd break a wooden spoon across my skin by beating me too viciously.

"Look what you made me do!" she'd snarl.

I'd be standing there, usually bruised and bleeding, having no idea what had set her off "*this* time." Wondering when she would finally kill me in a jealous rage. Wondering whether anyone would care if she did.

But no one cared about what they casually called "throwaway kids." Certainly not the people who were helping her abuse me in small and large ways.

How did people help her? Let me give you one example of a casual abuser. When I was sixteen, my wisdom teeth needed to be taken out. All four of them were impacted. This would normally require oral surgery and pain medication. But when I was in foster care, I was covered by MassHealth, so they did it out-patient in an overly brown surgery room. I'm a neurodiverse person, remember. Eight needles of Novocain: inner and outer side, top and bottom, left and right. Then he cut my gums open, applied pressure to the tooth until it broke, and dug out the broken tooth. Then he sewed up my gums for all four teeth and sent me on my way with Tylenol.

"Lest she become another person addicted to pain meds by the welfare system!"
Thanks, dude.

State-sponsored torture. And why? Because my foster mother told him my parents were addicts, and he had strong opinions he was going to work out on my flesh. What was the deal with that guy? Nothing, probably. That's how *a lot* of people are. Maybe he was an addict. Maybe his mother was. But that guy exacted his pound of flesh from a child and then went home and kissed his wife, I imagine, quite sure he had done the right thing, as "a good guy."

It's been that way throughout human history, but definitely all of my life as a foster kid.

Physical abuse is a way people work out their demons on children. That is a given. But more often than not, it's psychological abuse that does most of the work for an abuser, and they wield that well. Of course they do. It worked on *them first*. Making a child feel like she'd have no way out if she ran is a very powerful tool. Making her feel like everyone agrees that she's unworthy of any other life might work so well as to make a person harm herself with obsessive thoughts and self-hatred. I was doing the work *for* Karen, in the end.

And I stayed busy at that particular woodpile.

When I was seventeen, Neil's girlfriend was trying to make friends with the women and girls in the family. That's a thing. But Neil felt this girlfriend was above him socially and let Karen know it. And that logically meant the girlfriend was "above" Karen. It meant she was uncontrollable. So her plan for Neil's girlfriend had to be twofold. First, Karen had to bring her under her control. And, second, she had to keep her away from me. *That's how they do it.*

So what did Karen do? First, she told me Neil's girlfriend hated me because I wasn't Neil's *real* sister—the very thing that would hurt me the most. And she told his girlfriend *I* hated *her* and thought she was a "sl—t" who wasn't good enough for Neil.

Both accusations centered around subjects about which Karen would want more information, but that's the trick: make his girlfriend defend against the accusations, thus gaining even more intimate details than she'd want to provide to her about the subject, in this case her promiscuity or lack thereof.

I tell you this because I want you to see it as a blueprint. It usually looks like this.

Karen kept people she couldn't control apart so they would not team up against her. And she did so by acting as the go-between for two insecure people who weren't actually fighting each other, but her and themselves. Usually it would be about the only thing about them that shames them. And it would be about something they couldn't change *but would if they could.*

That's what a person fights against in these types of relationships. That's what a narcissistic abuser can see: the thing you hate the most about yourself. And then, in your shame, you accidentally reveal *even more* to them that they can use about (and against) you. You and your "enemies" of course. Which is really just *them.*

If you have a mother and you and your siblings have to use her as a go-between to communicate, you may also be dealing with a narcissist. They set up those conditions because it gives them the most power. They do this over and over with different variables. Narcissists aren't always smart, but they are effective.

You're welcome, children. Benefit from my years of therapy in hyper-obsessed-with-humans mode!

That's what I want you to take away from my story. How I survived this. That I did survive it. And you will, too, one awful step at a time. Just like I did.

I know how it hurts. I know some days you don't get out of bed from the pain of just the *memories.* I know it. It's hard.

But this is the one time I'll tell you, "If I can, you can."

This book wasn't about revenge. It was about *life.* My joy at being alive. And, honestly, if I still feel joy at the wonder of this life, still, then you know it's the real kind. Spark of Life joy. That's what you find at the very bottom of absolute hopelessness. Yourself and your spark. Your love for yourself. Your anger at their betrayal.

How do I know it's betrayal? It's always betrayal. Because the only people who can hurt you in that way are people who you *care about caring about you.*

This is my specific-genius space.

People.

To that end, if you are someone I wrote about in this book and you find yourself incensed about my finally telling this story to the world, I'd like to point out that I didn't tell anyone's worst thing.

And you know I know what they are. So keep toeing the line. Keep your nose clean of hurting other people. And you can keep your Darkest Secret.

Or don't. I write books for a living. You may test me at your earliest convenience. But remember what I said: A narcissist's bad deeds always carry the blueprint for their own destruction. Eventually, they are all the cause of their own end.

They may win a few battles, but they always lose the war.

So it's not, *not* about revenge.

But it's bigger than that. Because revenge is something you take against one person, usually on behalf of yourself. Out of anger.

I'm taking justice. Out of love. On behalf of all of us foster kids.

On behalf of all of the beaten children who never made it to tell their story.

To all our abusers:

Look what you made me do.

Thanks

As usual there are a lot of people to thank for this story finally coming together.

Thank you to my tremendous publishing team at Morgan James for believing in me.

Thank you to my writing coach and mentor, Nick, for always absorbing my anxiety with his wisdom.

Thank you to my editor, Catherine, for helping me finalize this manuscript.

Thank you to all the black-sheep ex-family members who sat for interviews with me.

Thank you to PBS.

Thank you to LeVar Burton.

Thank you to Rage Against the Machine.

Thank you to Mr. Dan Camilli.

Thank you to all the educators who saw me.

Thank you to all of you who became my friends and family in this life.

Thank you to my partner and sword-husband, Jay, who calms my storms and stays hot.

Thank you to my beautiful children, who heal me while they explore the world each day.

Thank you to all my communities, especially the LGBTQ+ community.

Thank you to the folks who were kind to me in Atlanta and helped me survive this story. I can because you did it first.

Thank you to Tyler Perry and Bert Weiss (again) for sharing their healing journeys that somehow found me in the dark of homelessness and abuse.

Thank you to folks like Glennon Doyle and Brené Brown for showing us how to learn hard things with grace.

Thank you to all of my lifelong cheerleaders.

Thank you to all of my friends who send me memes as a check-in style, especially Philip, Brandyn, and SamWise.

Thank you to my spiritual community, especially Jarrett, Heather Tharpe, Jamie Day, and Sarah Prescott.

Thank you to all the people who have spoken up for me in my life, like Jeff R., Kevin M., Christina, Teresa, Adrienne, Matt S., and all my honorary Gen X older siblings.

Thank you to my nanny, whom I could not live without.

Thank you. All of you. Truly.

About the Author

Diana Machado Ciruolo is a mother of two neurospicy kids, a DEI educator, and a social justice advocate. Her experiences growing up on the outside as a foster kid with neurodiversity have given her a unique understanding of humanness that informs her practice and her life. Di's passion is freeing other humans from the guilt and self-harm that can come from trauma and loss, and she has a love/hate relationship with public speaking. Di loves her made-family, Fleetwood Mac, trotty dogs, and standing in the ocean in her wellies year-round. Di tries each day to embody the Dolly Parton quote: "Find out who you are and do it on purpose." Di is married to her partner, Jay, and they enjoy a coastal grandmother lifestyle. You can connect with Di at her website www.diciruolo.com.

A free ebook edition
is available with the
purchase of this book.

To claim your free ebook edition:

1. Visit MorganJamesBOGO.com
2. Sign your name CLEARLY in the space
3. Complete the form and submit a photo of the entire copyright page
4. You or your friend can download the ebook to your preferred device

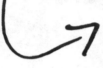

Morgan James
BOGO™

A **FREE** ebook edition is available for you or a friend with the purchase of this print book.

CLEARLY SIGN YOUR NAME ABOVE

Instructions to claim your free ebook edition:
1. Visit MorganJamesBOGO.com
2. Sign your name CLEARLY in the space above
3. Complete the form and submit a photo of this entire page
4. You or your friend can download the ebook to your preferred device

Print & Digital Together Forever.

Snap a photo

Free ebook

Read anywhere